Phyll to her Friends

Kathleen Swann

First Published in 2022

by Quantum Dot Press

ISBN: 978-1-912822-68-7

The story within this book was told to me by my mother and grandmother with additional information from relatives and friends. Other dates and details have been researched through Ancestry.com.

In memory of my mother
Phyllis Ashton, nee Gething
1917 – 2015
And for her family and friends

"Love recognises no barriers. It jumps hurdles, leaps fences,
penetrates walls to arrive at its destination full of hope"
Maya Angelou

Contents

List of Photos

Part 1

Elias's Early Years
- Daniel Gething
- Eliza Hallam
- Elias and Sarah, Dancing

The Payne Family
- Maria and her children in Catcliffe
- Elsie May Payne, Aged 13
- Eliza Payne and Frederick Hall, who married in 1919
- Elsie, Elias and Eliza

Married Life
- Crossley Carpets' record of Elsie Gething as a Flax Spinner

Part 2

Leaving
- Map of Woolshops showing Smith Street

Autumn 1926, The Attic
- Shroggs Road

List of Poetry

Introduction

Courage doesn't mean the absence of fear, but nevertheless when faced with almost impossible odds my mother didn't take the easier option to live with her father and grandparents, but stuck to what she believed was right, and took on several years of hardship and deprivation in order to support her mother.

My mother made many choices throughout her life which she always believed were well thought out choices, if not always the easiest ones, and which she felt made her life worthwhile. Her early years with my father, and as a mother, appeared humdrum and typical of many housewives in the post war years, but she was always fighting to recover the lost years of education and make up for the lack of security with which she had grown up.

She was a great reader and would always have a book at her side for any moment when she could pick it up and read another page, even in the kitchen when preparing meals. When she dusted and cleaned, she listened to the radio, and sang along to songs of the dance halls of her youth.

Her sense of independence and self-reliance continued throughout her life and gave her the determination to achieve some of her goals right through into her ninetieth decade. She had an inner strength, some may say stubbornness, born of many years of fighting to survive.

She loved her family and supported us, even when she didn't understand some of the choices we made. She knew we had to make our own way and develop our own self-reliance, but she was always there to listen and support.

Mum told me the events surrounding her early life over and over again in great detail, when I was a child and later as an adult. My grandmother, Elsie, told me some of her life when I visited her at Rye Lane. Many of the dates, and significant event details are the result of family history research on Ancestry.

I hope I've done you justice Mum.

Kathleen Swann
August, 2022

After reading Kathleen's absorbing account of her mother's life, I felt I knew Phyllis well enough to understand that she would never have wanted you to see her personal story as inspirational, although I certainly did. Her determination to leave behind the poverty of her childhood in order to create a stable and happy life for herself and her family tells us a great deal about what can be achieved through persistent effort and hard work, as well as reminding us of the strength and resilience that comes from being true to your core values.

History is brought to life here by exposing the realities of the times her forebears had to go through, making it possible to appreciate the true scale of Phyllis's achievements. The addition of photographs, personal comments from people who knew her, historical references and poems make this a fascinating read.

Although I was never fortunate enough to meet her, getting to know Phyllis through Kathleen's sensitive but honest biography has been a true pleasure.

Sheila Whitfield
August 2022

PART 1

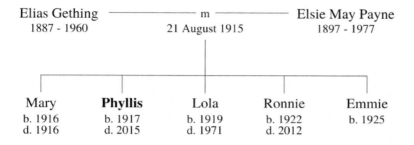

Elias Gething   m   Elsie May Payne
1887 - 1960   21 August 1915   1897 - 1977

Mary	**Phyllis**	Lola	Ronnie	Emmie
b. 1916	b. 1917	b. 1919	b. 1922	b. 1925
d. 1916	d. 2015	d. 1971	d. 2012	

Background & Early Childhood

If you'd ever met Phyllis, my mother, you would remember her. Her father's family had given her Celtic looks with large blue/grey eyes and, as she always said, her father's nose. She hadn't got her mother's curly red hair but just a gentle wave in her dark Welsh locks. But more than that, she would have greeted you warmly and asked questions in genuine interest about you. She would also have shared lots about herself, you would soon feel you had got to know her. Throughout her life she was generous, hardworking and loyal but she could also be forthright, honest and cutting. She didn't suffer fools gladly and her opinions were long held and mostly unmovable. However, if she felt your need was greater than hers or if something would give you pleasure, she would willingly share her possessions with you. Her stark life throughout her childhood had given her an insight into poverty, hunger and hardship which she never forgot, but which formed her stoical character and gave her an unsympathetic view of anyone who cheated the system or wasted opportunities.

My mother's story starts in the spring of 1917. The First World War had been raging for three years, thousands of young men had gone to fight, and many had died during the conflict. Women had taken on many of the men's jobs during this time despite having no level of social or financial equity with their husbands or brothers. Her father, Elias, was exempt from fighting on health grounds. He worked as a Dyer's Assistant in a woollen mill, Halifax being very much a mill town at the time. There were woollen mills, carpet mills and mills making parts for spinning and weaving machinery. These provided employment for a great number of the population, particularly women. Jobs in these mills were plentiful. My grandmother Elsie, and two of her sisters, worked in several different mills around the town throughout their lives.

......

Since Anglo Saxon times Yorkshire people had been fulling, spinning, weaving and dyeing wool at home, mainly to clothe their own family. Sheep grazed well on the hillsides of West Yorkshire and the water was soft for washing, scouring and dyeing the wool. The old ways stayed and grew into a commercial activity, trading both at home and abroad. With the Industrial Revolution Halifax, and the rest of West Yorkshire, expanded its number of mills and its wool production to manufacture blankets, carpets and heavyweight cloth for the textile industry. At the start of the twentieth century Halifax had in excess of 36 mills associated with the production of woollen cloth or carpets.

......

My mother was the second child of my grandparents, Elias and Elsie Gething. Sadly, their first daughter, Mary Eliza, died of pneumonia in the spring of 1916 at around 3 months old. By September Elsie was pregnant again and my mother was born on 30 May 1917. Mum's birth certificate says she was born at 17 Cedar Street, King Cross, a district of Halifax, although that is not one of the addresses listed by Elias on his divorce statement and may have been a temporary stay for the birth. It was common in those days for babies to be born at home unless the mother was unwell; a hospital birth was only considered if the home situation wasn't suitable or if there were any obvious signs of distress from the baby. Healthcare was not free; patients may have made voluntary payments into a local service or have paid what they could afford at the time. My grandmother claimed that she was attended by a midwife for my mother's birth, and this may have been because of the death of her first child. In many cases family members or local mothers would have helped a new mother bring her baby into the world.

The houses in these districts were generally 'back-to-back'. This meant that two terraces of houses were built together, each having only a front door which faced onto a different street. There was no electricity, so the walls had gas lights or candles for illumination. Rooms were often small and unheated except for the sitting room which had a coal fire. Coal fires were often 'damped down' at night in the hope that they would retain some heat and be easier to light in the morning. This was an unhealthy practice as the house could fill with smoke fumes, and it didn't improve the temperature in the rest of the house. On winter mornings there would be ice patterns on the inside of the windows and clothes kept in bedrooms were damp. The houses only had two bedrooms so eventually all the children shared a bed, which made the middle ones very cosy.

When they lived at Sykes Terrace, my grandmother's sister Lily lived in a similar house along the street with her daughter Elsie, who was just a bit older than my mother. The sisters were a support to each other, and the cousins were great friends and shared many times together throughout the whole of their lives. Lily's husband, Harry Glassbrook, was a soldier and was fighting in France at this time. Harry was killed on the Western Front in 1918 and so Lily became a war widow with a child to bring up. However, she did have a war widows' pension which helped her to cope and sometimes she would help my grandmother with food or money for coal.

Mum's sister, Lola Blanche, was born in October 1919. Elsie was, once again, confined to the house, although work was becoming harder for women to find as the men were returning to their pre-war jobs. The First World War had ended but many women were now war widows or coping with husbands who had returned badly injured and suffering from depression and shell shock, or PTSD as it is known today. The country was in the grip of Spanish Flu which caused the deaths of thousands of people. Many men who had survived the war succumbed to the terrible virus, because they were weak from injury and lack of nourishment as well as suffering from depression. This disease devastated the poorer, vulnerable families who worked in the crowded environments in the mills. The damp and cold living conditions made people susceptible to flu, chest complaints and Tuberculosis, which was rife.

My mother was a lively, bright child who captivated her father, Elias, with her singing and dancing. She had his colouring and vivacity for life. Elias spent lots of time with Mum when she was small. She would accompany him at weekends to many different community occasions, he liked to show her off to family and friends. Elias was one of ten children and there was much rivalry among them all to produce talented children. He was known in the area for his impersonation of Charlie Chaplin and used to dress up for the Infirmary Carnival as a character from Charlie's film, The Kid. Dressed as Charlie's sidekick from that film, Little Jackie Cougan, Mum would go with her father and the two of them would entertain the crowd with the side benefit of earning money which Elias would then spend liberally in the local pubs. This made him a colourful and popular character around the town. However, when her father was hard up he would abuse this relationship and take my mother into the local ale house with him. She would be dressed in her prettiest clothes with ribbons in her hair, then her father would get her to dance and sing on the tables. Customers would throw coins and that would pay for his beer and his bet on the dogs or horses.

Mum started school just before she was five and loved it, particularly English and mental arithmetic. She was enthusiastic in her desire to learn about everything and to join in classroom activities. She enjoyed reading, taking part in plays and poetry readings. She made friends in school and played happily in the playground, but as she got older, she became increasingly frustrated by the fact that her home life was falling apart and was reluctant to ask friends home.

The family grew with Mum's brother, Ronald (known as Ronnie), being born in 1922 and Emmie, in 1925. Elias worked as a Dyer's Labourer for George Armitage Ltd, Dyers and Finishers of Cotton Piecer Goods, and earned a regular wage, but this didn't often get to Elsie's purse. The pregnancies and difficulty with childcare made it hard for Elsie to work, although she did some shifts in the mills when she could, but this put an added pressure on my mother. Mum had to stay at home and look after the young children when they were sick. She already dressed the younger ones in the morning before she went to school and gave them breakfast, usually bread and margarine, often giving up her own share to feed them. When they were old enough to go to school she took them with her and brought them home at night. Mum helped with the washing, drying and sorting of clothes, keeping the house clean and running errands. Her childhood was drowned in responsibility.

Growing up

Dance for daddy he said
in the bright noisy bar,
so she tapped her toes
twirled on the table
in a pale pink cotton dress,
as coins landed at her feet.

Another round landlord, he shouted
smiling at the assembled crowd
I'm thirsty Daddy she whispered,
run home to your mother he snarled,
as the pub door slammed

          silence
               and loneliness
                    enveloped her.

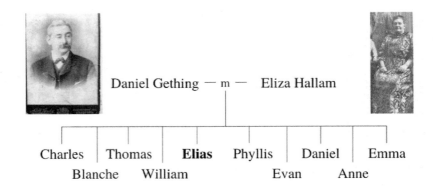

Daniel Gething — m — Eliza Hallam

Charles | Thomas | **Elias** | Phyllis | Daniel | Emma
Blanche | William | | Evan | Anne

Elias's Early Years

My grandfather Elias was born on 28 February 1888. I have learned a lot of what I know about his early life from his sons and daughters. However, writing his story isn't straightforward for me. Elias's children have differing views of him as a father, although they all say he was never violent towards them. I accept that memories become distorted with time and, as children, events can become overinflated in the mind, and sometimes we remember more about what we have been told rather than what actually happened. In this account I have tried to balance views from several different people who knew Elias. I have taken the words of various family members at face value and tried not to make assumptions about what might have happened.

Sadly, I don't remember my grandfather as we moved away from Halifax when I was only eighteen months old, so I didn't have the opportunity to get to know him or to form my own opinions. Our visits back to Halifax were rare and for short periods in those early days. Travel was expensive, we didn't have a car, and there were many relatives and friends to visit. As you will see, my mother wasn't welcome at her father's house. On our occasional trips to see my grandmother and aunts during the 1950s, Mum would try and 'bump into' her father when he was alone. After his retirement he could often be found in King Cross, where the family butcher's shop was still thriving. Mum would walk down the high street hoping to see him without coming across his second wife or his other family members. It would be many years before she was prepared to meet her half-sisters and brother.

Elias's parents, Daniel and Eliza, had moved from South Wales to Halifax sometime between 1882 and 1886. Their first four children were born in Abedare but they had a further six children in Halifax. Daniel had been a blacksmith in Wales, but I can only assume that they moved to West Yorkshire for work as there weren't any other family members in Halifax at that time. I think he thought that a blacksmith's skills would be useful in mending the machinery in the mills around the area. This didn't work out, and his health was deteriorating, Daniel eventually started a family butcher's shop in King Cross.

Elias was the fifth of the ten children and his childhood wasn't easy. He was born partially deaf, and due to a problem with his vocal chords, he was unable to speak. He did attend Pellon Lane junior school with his siblings, but he sat silently in the class, taking in what was going on but not taking part in the lessons. When he was thirteen, he got a place at Parkinson Lane Special School but, like most children at that time, he left school aged fourteen so he didn't receive any constructive special teaching and left school unable to either read or write.

However, he made up for his lack of literacy by having a head for numbers. He could work out betting odds in his head like lightening although that didn't mean he won any more frequently. He was a keen follower of both horse and dog racing, being a regular at the dog track in Halifax.

When Elias was fifteen, his Aunt Margaret and Uncle Daniel paid for him to have an operation on his vocal chords to help him to speak. This was partially successful although he still had problems with sounds, particularly S, which he pronounced as a T. His daughter's name, Zera, he pronounced as Tera, his wife, Sarah as Terah. He would use expressions like, "my wife's sister's husband" instead of "my brother-in-law" or "my brother's wife's son" instead of "my nephew". The family claim some of his first intelligible words were swear words when he was kicked whilst playing football.

Despite his difficulty with speech, he was a very sociable young man, he enjoyed taking part in physical sports. During his teenage years he became the local amateur roller-skating champion and junior amateur boxing champion. He regularly beat his cousins and his brother, Evan, in boxing competitions. The vicar of the local church, St Jude's, was a very autocratic man who rode around on a horse and used his whip to move people out of his way. When Elias refused to be pushed around, the vicar got off his horse and said "I'll teach you how to behave my man", and put up his fists, whereupon Elias knocked him straight through a butcher's shop window, much to the delight of the bystanders. The vicar was said to be more careful about pushing people around after that.

I am particularly sorry I didn't see him dance, because he was an extremely accomplished ballroom dancer. Elias had learned to dance in the dance halls of Halifax but on a day trip to Blackpool he discovered the Tower Ballroom. Throughout his adult life he went to Blackpool several times a year, where he danced and gave lessons. Blackpool Tower took on additional teachers during the summer holidays in the 20s and 30s. The money he earned paid for a family holiday in Blackpool each year.

Elias and Sarah, Dancing

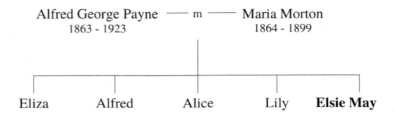

Alfred George Payne ⸺ m ⸺ Maria Morton
1863 - 1923   1864 - 1899

Eliza   Alfred   Alice   Lily   **Elsie May**

The Payne Family

Elsie May Payne, my grandmother, was born on 5 February1897, the youngest of five children, four girls and a boy. The family were living in Frederick Street in Catcliffe, South Yorkshire. My grandmother had no memory of her mother, Maria. She was only two years old when Maria died in childbirth in October 1899. This was not an uncommon occurrence in those days, but none the less heart-breaking, and had a lasting effect on the lives of the other children and the wider family.

Since I can't find any record of a live birth for that date, I can only assume that the child was stillborn or died during the birth. Maria's death certificate records that she 'died of exhaustion during childbirth'. Her husband, Alfred was with her and 'witnessed her death'. I can only imagine how painful this must have been for him.

The remaining five children were brought up by their father, Alfred, and maternal grandmother, Charlotte, who must have been a formidable presence as she was already

helping out with these grandchildren and others from her other children. Alfred had moved to South Yorkshire from Northumberland, where he had been a glass bottle blower but was now working as a miner. His wider family were still in Northumberland.

Maria & her children in Catcliffe

Elsie was a redhead with blue eyes, a freckled complexion and thick, tight curly hair which knotted easily and was hard to manage. When she felt it was getting too long she used to cut it by pulling the ringlets straight and just cutting to the length she wanted. Her hair would just bounce back into curls.

Elsie May Payne, Aged 13

By 1901 the older children were working. Elsie's oldest sister, Eliza, had left home and was working as a maid. She was 16 and it was very common for girls to find a position as a domestic servant. This provided the young woman with a home and pay and took the burden from the rest of the household. Initially she worked in Catcliffe, but then she moved to Blackpool where she had found a position in a large house on Raikes Road. She eventually married Frederick Hall in 1919 and in 1920 they had a daughter, Ethel Roma. Eliza died in Blackpool in 1964 aged 78.

Eliza Payne and Frederick Hall, who married in 1919

Her brother, Alfred, went to work in the South Yorkshire mines, first as a lamp carrier and then as a hewer. The hewer in a mine was trained to recognise and cut the coal or ore from the seam and be able to separate it from the worthless rocks around. He married Beatrice in 1910 and had one son, Samuel. The family remained in South Yorkshire and Alfred died in 1974 aged 86.

In order to share childcare and work in the mills, Alice moved to Halifax in 1917 to live with her sister, Lily, following the birth of her illegitimate daughter, whom she also named Alice. Lily's husband, Harry, was away fighting in

France and was ultimately killed in 1918. Alice eventually met and married William Craven in July 1921 and he took on her daughter Alice.

Lily was the sister who stayed closest to Elsie May throughout her life. They supported each other in difficult times, although when Lily remarried this wasn't as easy as her second husband was not so keen on Elsie May and her lifestyle.

Elsie, Elias and Eliza

Schooling was basic in the early 1900s, particularly for girls. Lessons were focused on domestic skills rather than academic achievement. Elsie did learn to read and write, but she was not confident, and her grasp of maths was minimal. Money in the home in Catcliffe was tight, and work in the village was hard to find, particularly for girls, so when Elsie was thirteen, her sister, Eliza, found her a position as a maid on the same road as herself in Blackpool.

Elsie was taken on as a general maid, and her duties included cleaning out the fire grates, fetching coal and lighting the fires. Her tasks included dusting, sweeping, washing floors, general cleaning and doing the laundry. She became a trusted maid and helped to polish the silver, but this was under supervision as she was so young. She ran errands for the more experienced staff working in the house. She got up every morning between five thirty and six o'clock and worked until nine or ten at night for six days a week. It was a hard life but a fair one, she was provided with a uniform, was fed in the kitchen with the other staff and had one day off a week. Elsie stayed here for approximately four years.

During this time, either in Blackpool or when visiting her sister in Halifax, she met Elias Gething and by 1914 she had moved to Luddenden Foot in Halifax where her sister Lily was working in the mills.

Elsie always said what a wonderful dancer Elias was and how he, quite literally, swept her off her feet. Elsie and Elias were married on August 21st 1915, in the parish church in Luddenden Foot. Although the marriage certificate says Elsie was 21, in fact she was eighteen and Elias was 27. The certificate names her father as Frederick. He was actually Alfred, but known as Fred, so I think an assumption was made about his name. He wasn't present at the wedding. Elias's sister, Annie, stood as a witness and Elsie was four months pregnant. Initially the couple lived at the Brewery House, Cote Hill, they then moved to Green Head in Norland.

Married Life

This is 1915 and World War 1 was in full swing. There were many young men, including members of both families, signing up and going off to fight in unknown and unimaginable conditions. Elias, my grandfather, was exempt from fighting. His poor hearing and inability to communicate properly made him unsuitable for military service so he continued to work as an Apprentice Dyer in one of the woollen mills. Elsie was taken on as a 'flax spinner' in Crossley's carpet factory in Halifax in 1915 and continued to work there off and on until 1929.

*Crossley Carpets' record of Elsie Gething as
a flax spinner*

She was now living in a strange town and, although she had her older sister Lily in Halifax, in January 1916 she had to cope with the birth of her first child followed by the death of this daughter, Mary Eliza, from bronchial pneumonia at just three months old. Elias worked long hours and still liked to have his nights out with his friends and brothers. Elsie felt lost and lonely, especially when her young baby became ill. Her mother-in-law, Eliza, had been widowed at the age of 50, and her second husband was a drunkard, so she worked long, hard hours in the butcher's shop to keep her family going and didn't have much time to help Elsie and Elias.

The death of a child under one was not uncommon. The infant mortality rate in 1915 was 162.78 meaning that approximately 163 children in 1000 died before they reached five years old. Houses were cold and damp and my grandparents lived in a small terraced house, the mill chimneys gave off dirty emissions and the air quality was poor. There were no antibiotics and visits to the doctor cost money. Just because infant deaths happened to many couples, it did not make the heartache and sense of loss any the less. Elsie became pregnant again quickly and had Phyllis in 1917, Lola in 1919, Ronnie in 1922 and Emmie in 1925. Every day was a fight, she was always weary and felt dragged down by her domestic life.

The heartache of losing their first child and then the strain of having four children in fairly quick succession cannot be underestimated in contributing to the breakdown of their marriage. Elsie would complain bitterly when Elias came home after a night out, but it was unforgivable of my grandfather to keep money for his own entertainment when his children were going hungry. Young women around the area would often stop Elsie and tell her what a good dancer her husband was and how they had spent a wonderful evening in his company. Elsie was kept short of money and, despite the family having a butcher's shop, she was often scratching around to feed her children and herself. Elsie worked in the mill when she could get shifts and childcare, but she also looked for companionship and love in these places too, something that was in short supply at home.

My mother had already taken on the role of getting the younger children washed, undressed and into bed at night, but if her father wasn't home by her bedtime, she would lie under the covers fully dressed, knowing that when he came home there would be trouble. Elias would arrive home drunk and demand a meal, which might or might not be available depending on whether Elsie had any money. She would stand up for herself, but if she answered him back, he would invariably hit her. My mother would sneak out and run down the street to Elsie's sister, Lily, to get her to come and break up the fight. The more children Elsie had, the less money there was available and the worse this abuse became. Elias never hit his children, but my mum was frightened about what he might do to Elsie.

Black eyes and bruised arms were often seen on women in those days, but Mum had a strong sense that life shouldn't be that way, and she gradually withdrew from talking to her father. Elias had spent a lot of time with Phyllis when she was younger, and he resented this behaviour, so he and Phyllis became increasingly at odds with each other. He would try and get her to go for a walk with him or offer to take her to visit cousins, but she would refuse and say she preferred to play with her sister and brother. Elias blamed Elsie for encouraging this behaviour and took it out on the family by going out more.

In 1926 Elsie decided to leave Elias. She knew his mother and the wider family would help him with the children, and that there would be money to feed and clothe them, which she had struggled to do. There was work to be had in the mills, but they were long hours, mostly twelve hour shifts from early morning, and this made looking after small children on her own almost impossible.

Elsie's young life had been shaped by the fact that her father had been forced to take on the care of his five children when his wife, Maria, died, so Elsie had an expectation that her husband would be supportive with the children in the same way. Her childhood was one where her grandmother, older sisters and aunts had helped with mending, washing clothes and cooking family meals. The five siblings and their cousins were all looked after together. It hadn't been a bad life but there was no one-to-one affection or individual attention. Life had been all about the practicalities of survival. Elsie knew how to deal with these but wanted love, kindness and support from Elias. It wasn't forthcoming.

PART 2

Leaving

Easter 1926 had been a hard time with Elias out drinking dancing and betting on the dogs. Elsie was desperate and frightened. She had been having an affair with Edward Prescott and she was pregnant. Elsie knew she had to leave soon and was worried what to do about her children. The risks she ran if Elias found out that she was leaving were many, he would certainly give her a beating but she didn't know if he would also take it out on the children, so Elsie had to plan it carefully. She knew she would have to leave the children in order to work to keep herself.

She prepared to go into hiding with the intention of leaving her new home only to go to work. She had talked to her sisters, Lily and Alice, about what she was doing, and they were prepared to look after the children short term, but couldn't take four of them on permanently, they had their own children to keep. Besides they didn't want to have to deal with Elias after Elsie left. Mum knew that Elsie was planning something, because she had watched the clean clothes going into a bag under the bed rather than in the drawer. She kept sitting the children on her knee and cuddling them more frequently. Mum eventually confronted her, and she explained that she couldn't take any more of Elias's behaviour and that she was moving out. She assured Mum that their father and grandparents would look after them all and she was adamant that she would come back for them when she had somewhere safe to live and could earn enough money to keep them. This was a naivety that showed Elsie's lack of understanding of many things in the world. There was very little hope of a woman's mill wages paying enough to keep four children, as well as pay for childcare and rent a house big enough for them all. There was little state help at this time, and if Elsie didn't pay her rent, she, and her children would end up in the workhouse. Mum was adamant that she would not go with her father, and she threatened to run away, so after many scenes and tears, Elsie took pity on her and agreed to take her. Mum was independent enough to look after herself, and Elsie knew her well enough to know that she was capable of causing all sorts of aggravation if she was unhappy.

On the 1st of May 1926, Elsie and Mum packed what they could carry, took Emmie to Lily, who would also take in the other children when they came back from school, and they set off to walk to the other side of town into the slum area called Woolshops.

......

Woolshops in Halifax is believed to be the only district in the world with this name. The name is said to derive from the traders, or staplers, who sold wool by the stone rather than by the bale. A 'staple' is a measure of wool and the reason staplers sold wool in these small amounts was because of the volume of cloth produced in individual homes. The area dates back to medieval times and is mentioned in the 1555 Act of Parliament.

......

Elsie had found a room in a Rooming House, or Common Lodging House. Rooming houses provided one room per family with a sink, a shelf or cupboard, a single gas ring, gas lights on two walls, bare floorboards and no heating or furniture. There was a fireplace, but their chimney was dripping soot and obviously needed sweeping. There was one bathroom for the whole building which might consist of twelve or fifteen families. The house bathroom had a tin bath, a toilet and a washbasin on a bare floor. There was no hot water provided. Tenants were responsible for almost everything in these rooms because landlords were not obliged to provide anything other than a basic room.

Map of Woolshops showing Smith Street

Elsie and Mum's room was on the first floor at the end of a long corridor. This corridor had no lighting. The room to their right had two young men suffering from Tuberculosis (TB) so the coughing and spitting continued day and night. The other side was occupied by an elderly couple who were kind to Elsie and Mum, but they had hit hard times through ill health and had hardly anything themselves. The room underneath was used by three prostitutes. These girls were relatively well off and had some furniture and a gas heater. This was to be a life saver to my mother when she was starving and frozen on winter nights.

......

They arrived in Smith Street in Woolshops with just the few clothes they had packed and some newspapers which Elsie had been collecting for a couple of weeks. Newspaper is relatively cheap and a very effective insulating material. Mum's first task was to go to the market and buy a bucket to put in the corner of the room for a toilet, and some more newspapers. They used torn-up newspaper as toilet paper, because it was cheaper, and softer than the hard, scratchy paper sold as toilet roll. A piece of newspaper would be burnt in the bucket each day to mask the smell.

Elsie had packed a piece of carbolic soap to enable them to scrub the room and a piece of toilet soap for washing. The two of them worked together all day to clean the room thoroughly and pinned some of Elsie's old scarves over the windows for some privacy. There were other old, tall buildings, close by and the windows faced into each other. Elsie carefully laid newspaper on the floor in one corner of the room and told Mum this was where they would sleep. It would be their bed for many months to come. They had taken their winter coats and boots and slept fully clothed and covered by their coats. Elsie had collected some shillings and she put them into an old tin for the gas meter, the only source of power for their cooking or lighting. Mum said she didn't have a full night's sleep for weeks it was so hard and cold, even with the newspaper.

Their days would begin with an all over wash, in lukewarm water if there was enough money for gas to boil the kettle, or, if not, in cold water. Breakfast was a slice of bread spread with dripping or margarine, butter and jam being too expensive. Elsie would be gone before six and Mum would make her way to school for nine o'clock. There were no school lunches, so if there was any spare bread, she would take a slice spread with dripping, but that would be all she would eat until Elsie arrived home in the evening. It was a good day for Mum when one of the prostitutes came home and found her sitting on the doorstep, they would often buy her a bag of chips from the chip-shop at the end of the street.

Some days Elsie and Mum would barely see anything of each other, but their relationship was a companionable one. They worked hard together to keep the room and themselves clean, they made use of every scrap of food they bought, ekeing it out from payday to payday. Heat and light only being used when it was absolutely necessary. On Sundays, if it was fine, they would go for a walk together, in summer they would pick bilberries on the moor and Elsie would cover them with a breadcrumb-crust for a tea-time treat.

Elsie continued to work for Crossley's, working at least twelve-hour shifts and taking on any overtime that was offered. She could expect to earn twenty-five shillings (£1.25) for a twelve-hour shift. At least half of this wage would be spent on rent, the other half would have to pay for everything else. Elsie's long working hours meant that Mum was on her own both before she went to school and when she came home. If it was fine and light, she would sometimes walk over to Shroggs Road, where her brother and sisters lived, and watch them playing in the yard. She just wanted to check that they were alright and then she could tell her mother. It made her sad that she could never approach them or speak to them at this time, she was afraid of being chased away. It emphasised the loneliness she felt spending the long days on her own. Elsie felt very guilty leaving them, especially Emmie, but there was no way she could have looked after them and work as well. She always said she did it out of love for them, but that must have been hard for children so young to understand and for her to rationalise. Her relationship with these children was always tenuous and strained throughout her life.

Food was meagre and very basic. On pay day Elsie would buy a cheap piece of meat on the bone for Sunday lunch. She would boil it on the gas ring with onion and vegetables. Then during the week, she would make soup from the bones by adding potatoes or vegetables. Eggs could be bought singly, so with flour and water or a little milk if they had any, Yorkshire pudding could be made in a frying pan on the gas ring. Elsie would make the batter, a little thicker than normal, then drop a large tablespoonful into hot dripping saved from the weekend meat, the puddings would rise up round the edges and cook like a thick pancake in the middle. They would eat this with any left-over meat or vegetables. Fish was too expensive, but mussels were cheap, and Elsie would boil up a pan of mussels with wild herbs and vegetables. Served with a slice of fresh bread this made a tasty and filling meal. Many days they ate only bread and broth. Mum continued to make 'frying pan' Yorkshire Pudding when I was a child, I was a teenager before I ate a traditional Yorkshire Pudding.

Initially they lived in fear of being found by Elias, so they didn't go out except to work and school. Even then they spent their journeys watching behind them for fear of being followed by one of the numerous Gething family members and reported to Elias. At the end of May, when it was my mother's ninth birthday, Lily's daughter, also named Elsie and also nine, rode her child's bike, a fairy cycle my mother remembered, into the area looking for Mum. It was the one treat of her birthday and the two of them sat on the doorstep and talked for an hour before Cousin Elsie had to ride home again. My mother talked about that act of kindness repeatedly. Such a small thing but it meant so much to her.

Elias believed that Elsie had gone to live with Edward Prescott and it suited Elsie to let this be the case. Elias did go looking for Elsie and met Edward at his home. An argument ensued, and there was talk of a fight but in the end Elias left, as Elsie was clearly not there.

Mum wept when she talked about these days. They lived in these awful conditions for almost ten years. After four years, when Mum started full time work, the deprivation eased a little but there were two other children to look after by then, so it was only a small improvement. The cold and the malnutrition took its toll on their health for many years. In fact, I think it affected Mum's health for the rest of her life although it improved significantly when she married Dad. She suffered from poor circulation, which gave her other conditions and made her always feel the cold. Mum lived in rented accommodation all her life and was always grateful for the better conditions provided by good landlords and by my father's ability to decorate, make furniture and repair all manner of things.

Autumn 1926, The Attic

Elsie continued to work as many hours as she could to earn enough to pay the rent and feed the two of them, whilst getting ever heavier with her pregnancy. Her stomach was bound with strips of fabric to hide her shape for as long as possible. Being told to stop work early was her inherent fear; she planned to work until her labour started or her waters broke. That way she would lose the least amount of money, and hopefully, her employer would take her back after the birth. There was no account taken of how a child might be looked after, no crèche or nursery provision, so Elsie just had to work that out for herself, because the mill owners just wanted the carpets produced on time. She was a popular employee, always clean and tidy and never late for a shift. She didn't give backchat and worked hard, helping other workers if they were struggling.

The owner of the mill knew Elsie found things financially hard. She was always one of the first to volunteer to work overtime, and so he asked if her daughter was old enough to take on domestic work. Elsie told him she was at school all week, although she also knew that there would soon be a baby for her to look after. Elsie had no choice but to rely on Mum for childcare, and Mum knew this was the price she paid for living with her mother rather than her father.

When Elsie told Mum about the possibility of work at the Crossley house, Mum put on her tidiest clothes and went round to the house to ask if there was any Saturday work.

She was offered the job of cleaning the approach to the big house at a rate of 4d for scrubbing all the steps up to the house and donkey stoning the edges. This she did, reliably, apart from her time in the attic, in all weathers throughout the year. Eventually, she was asked by the owners of one or two other large houses to scrub steps, and this hard-earned income was a welcome contribution towards food and fuel. The work had to be finished by lunchtime in case the owners were expecting visitors, so every Saturday morning, bright and early, Mum would be scrubbing steps in all weathers. If she was lucky, the maid would bring her warm water, but sometimes it was freezing cold water from the scullery tap. Despite the additional income there still wasn't any spare money for furniture, and the two of them continued to sleep on newspaper covered by coats all through that year.

By November it was obvious, even to my mother, that Elsie was heavily pregnant and not far from giving birth. When Elsie went into labour she told Mum to go to her grandmother (Elias's mother) and ask her to take her in for two weeks. My mother resisted this, but after spending one night in the cold, dark room on her own, she made her way across town to Shroggs Road, her grandmother's house and knocked on the door. Her grandmother, Eliza, had been widowed in 1905 and had, unwisely, remarried one of her first husband's friends, John Tipling, a man who turned out to be lazy and a drunkard. He heard Eliza talking to my mother on the doorstep and came out to threaten Mum with his belt, telling her to go back to her 'no-good' mother. He wasn't keen on having to look after Elias's children at all, and didn't want another one around. Eliza followed Mum into the lane and took pity on her.

January 1953 ? Shroggs Road

Shroggs Road, January 1953

She told her to go round to the back of the house and wait for her. What seemed like hours later, Eliza came out with a blanket, wrapped Mum up, and took her secretly up to the attic. The attic was dark, only lit by a small skylight during the day and a torch her grandmother gave her for night time. That first night was so cold, as Mum only had a thin dress and coat on. The next day Eliza brought a cushion and an extra blanket to keep her warm, but it was a very inhospitable place. The rafters creaked, and the noise of birds on the roof and in the chimneys worried Mum, she was afraid that there were rats. It was a dirty, spidery environment with no comfortable place to sit or lie. Mum stayed up there for over three weeks. Eliza would bring her bread and cold meat or a cup of hot soup when there was no one else in the house. She had a bowl for a toilet which Eliza emptied infrequently.

Mum had no idea what was happening to her mother or what would happen to her if John, or her father (Elias), heard her and caught her. She had nothing to do all day, she didn't dare make any noise, and it being November/December, the dark nights were long. Mum practised her spellings in her head and created an imagined life for herself around the stories she had read at school, of course she didn't have any books at home. She said it was the longest three weeks of her life, and she was afraid she might have to stay up in the attic forever if her mother didn't come back for her.

Eventually Eliza heard, from Lily, that Elsie was back home and asking for Phyllis, so, just as secretively, my mother was sneaked out of the attic into the back lane and left to find her way back to Woolshops. She hadn't had more than a face wash with a damp flannel or a change of clothes in all that time. She was ashamed of the state she was in, because both she and her mother washed themselves from head to toe every day and tried to keep their clothes clean and fresh. Carbolic soap was cheap and cold water didn't cost much.

What my mother didn't know at the time, was that Elsie had given birth to a little boy at the end of November called Joseph Edward, named after his father. Joseph had lived for less than a month and died of pneumonia. Elsie had been back at Smithy Street in Woolshops since her discharge from hospital, and after Joseph died, she asked Lily to let Eliza know that Phyllis could come home. Elsie didn't know that Mum had been hidden in the attic, she'd assumed that Eliza would take her in with the other children. The late autumn was very cold and snowy in 1926 and Elsie had wrapped Joseph in newspaper and a blanket that she took home with her from the hospital. But it was too cold and damp for a small baby, and as Elsie herself was badly nourished, she found it hard to feed him. Joseph died on 13 December 1926

Mum came home dirty and frightened. There was little money as Elsie had been unable to work and Mum hadn't been to her Saturday jobs. She felt very guilty, and the first thing she did, after she had cleaned herself up and dressed in clean clothes, was go and apologise, scrub the steps and promise faithfully to be back the following week. Christmas came and went unmarked with little warmth, no gifts and very meagre food.

Getting a Second Job

The winter of 1926 was wet and windy right through into the spring of 1927. My mother continued to look after herself for long hours before and after school. She was curious about what a flax spinner did and why Elsie had to work so many hours, so one Saturday afternoon Elsie took Mum into the mill to see what it was like and what she actually did. Mum was appalled at the noise of the machinery, the clattering of the loom and shuttles was unbearable, and the work looked so boring she vowed never to work in a place like that. The women talked to each other in a mixture of sign language and speaking with exaggerated mouth movements. Elsie continued to talk in this way throughout her life. This revelation did make Mum appreciate how hard Elsie worked for her money, but it also made her think more seriously about what she might be able to do after school.

In the spring of 1927 one of the milliners in town put a notice in the window asking for someone to deliver hats. Mum ran home and asked her mother if she could apply, Elsie agreed, took some money from the 'gas tin' and together they went to the Salvation Army shop to get a warm coat and a beret. Mum, dressed in her 'new clothes', went to the shop to apply for the job. Mum was only ten, and the manager had been looking for someone older, but he was so impressed with her enthusiasm and her smart appearance that he gave her the job and for the next four years my mother delivered hats on Saturdays and, sometimes, after school to the well-dressed ladies of Halifax. Mum walked to all the smart areas of town, up and down long drives and up many of the steepest hills in the town. She earned her wage, and sometimes got a tip from the hat owner. She handed all this money over to her mother. It meant that they could use the gas a little bit more often, buy more wood or coal for the fire and some meat through the week. This would be scrag end or offal but it made hot, tasty meals. The cheapest cuts of meat were liver, kidneys, heart and products made from the rubbish bits of meat cut from the leaner joints. The butcher would sometimes wrap up some bones to go with the meat and Elsie would cook them for broth. If there were any vegetables or lentils she made a tasty soup.

The young prostitutes who worked in the ground floor room were kind to Mum. If they didn't have any clients, they would take her into their room and put the heater on. She would be treated to a bag of chips so that when she went home, warm and with a full stomach, she would curl up under her coat and sleep.

Despite the difficult circumstances in which they lived, Mum was a well-mannered, honest, cheerful child who smiled and always spoke politely to the local shopkeepers and market traders. She was a popular figure in the area. She used her charm to ask for old orange boxes or vegetable boxes from the shopkeepers, and the two of them used these for stools to sit on, shelves for storing things or small tables to put food on. They were still managing with two cups, plates, knives, forks and spoons. Elsie's sister, Lily, gave them two army blankets and an old eiderdown which, when put together on the floor, served as a softer, warmer bed.

The local Salvation Army were a great source of support and help to the community, and for a few pence provided good quality, second hand clothes. Many of these items had been donated by the mill owners' wives or occupants of the larger more affluent homes, and were generally well made from good quality fabric. However, as the summer wore on, it soon became apparent that Elsie was pregnant again. When the time came for her to give birth, Mum didn't go to her grandmother's. She was too frightened and didn't want to give up her earnings. She stayed on her own and her mother was only away for three days.

On 5 December 1927 Elsie gave birth to a little girl, Kathleen, in St Luke's Hospital. Kathleen's birth certificate has no named father, however it is fairly certain that Edward Prescott was the father, as he was cited as the co-respondent in Elsie and Elias's divorce in 1928/9. Edward disappeared from Elsie's life shortly after Kathleen's birth and took no part in her upbringing. Elsie took two weeks off work and then left my mother to look after Kathleen whilst she went back to the mill. Christmas was a very lean affair again and only the kindness of the local shopkeepers provided them with any food for Christmas Day.

'Mother' before her time

Elsie would try to feed Kathleen three times during the day; before she went to work, then again if Mum wheeled the pram up to the factory at lunch time, and again when she came back from work. However, Elsie was so poorly nourished that her milk was not very satisfying for Kathleen. Sugar water from a spoon had to suffice when she cried with hunger. Elsie had acquired some old towelling fabric from the off-cuts at one of the mills, and torn into squares they acted as nappies. Terry nappies were too expensive, but towelling worked well. They had to be scrubbed in the sink and dried on a string line across the room. This contributed to the continuous earthy smell and damp atmosphere in the room.

An old pram, given by one of the mill owner's wives, gave Kathleen somewhere to sleep and kept some of the draughts away from her. Mum had been scrubbing steps regularly for a family with growing children, and she was sometimes given a hot drink on cold mornings. She chatted to the scullery maid as she drank her tea and told her that her mother was expecting another baby. Mabel, the maid, said they were getting rid of some baby things and asked her mistress if Phyllis's mother could have the pram, so Mum wheeled the pram home across town and surprised Elsie. This one kind gesture made life a lot easier. It enabled Mum to take Kathleen to Lily's one or two days a week which meant she could go to school. If there was a hat to deliver after school Kathleen could be taken with her during the week. However, the winter of 1927/8 was very wet and windy, so pushing a pram and keeping a new hat in a pristine box clean and dry was quite a challenge. Added to the fact that both Mum and Kathleen were very undernourished, it is a wonder they didn't succumb to some terrible disease throughout this winter. Solid food for Kathleen for many weeks was stale bread when it had gone hard. This gave her something to chew on when she was teething. Surprisingly Kathleen did thrive and, with help from Lily and the kindly couple next door, my mother managed to keep the attendance officer at bay and continue some degree of studying.

Mum kept up her two jobs, often by taking Kathleen with her but mostly at weekends when Elsie was at home. On summer days, when Kathleen was at Lily's, Mum would go and collect bilberries on the moor after school. This extra food was a welcome addition and a great source of vitamins. She loved the clean air and feeling of freedom up on the moor and looking down over the town.

On rare days when there was no work, and the weather was warm Elsie and Mum would put Kathleen in the pram and walk to the local park. It was a peaceful place filled with beautiful flower beds and benches to sit and admire the lake and the ducks. It cost nothing and was as near to a 'holiday' as either of them had in those days. These times were precious to my Mum, they gave her time to talk to her mother and try to understand how they might get out of this terrible poverty. Elsie wasn't highly educated but she did understand that her own childhood had been fractured, and that she hadn't had a close relationship with any female adult. Elsie tried hard to give Mum more, but the lack of money always dragged them back to the basics of life taking priority.

However, Elsie also needed love and companionship, and this resulted in pregnancies which weakened her body and either ended in miscarriage or another child to feed.

Phyllis and Kathleen in 1929

By the late summer of 1929 it was obvious that Elsie was pregnant again. This event was the one thing which I heard Mum criticise about her mother. The thought of having to look after another baby and find the money to feed and clothe another person was very depressing, and almost more than Mum could bear. She didn't understand how Elsie could be so thoughtless and unthinking. Kathleen was almost two years old, and becoming a bit more independent, which made it easier to find babysitters and for Mum to go to school more frequently. Life was getting a little bit easier, they had managed to get a bed from the Salvation Army and although all three of them had to share it, it was warmer than sleeping on the floor. Mum had been thinking that the coming winter might be more manageable, but the thought of another baby to look after just depressed her.

Life had fallen into a routine. Kathleen was looked after by someone else for about three days a week and by Mum for two days, and Elsie was usually at home on Saturday afternoons, although she did occasionally work on Saturday for overtime. This meant that Mum had to scrub steps in double quick time and was sometimes delivering hats as it was going dark. The money wasn't a luxury, but it meant the rent was always paid on time, and despite the hard times there was always something to eat now, even if it was bone broth and stale bread. It was quite a treat if they bought an apple, sliced it thinly onto white bread and sprinkled a few grains of sugar over, this made a delicious sandwich for tea. I once took my mother round our local workhouse museum, and when we got to the display of food rations for each meal, she said " If I'd had that much food to eat in a day, I would have thought I was in heaven".

Baby minding again

On 12 December 1929 Elsie gave birth to another girl, Joyce, and so my mother's round of caring for a baby began again. Joyce was a small baby and always seemed to have a sniffle. They kept her as warm as they could and wrapped her in a cloth in the pram lined with newspaper. Kathleen objected, as she thought it was her pram. If Mum put both children in the pram together, Kathleen would nip Joyce to make her cry, then sit there with 'a butter wouldn't melt in her mouth' smile on her lips. The difficulty of getting the pram up a flight of stairs was hard enough without a baby and a toddler to carry as well. Mum would often wait for a burly-looking man to come down the street and then enlist his help to carry the pram or the children up the stairs. She would flash her blue eyes and look helpless in the hope that he would take pity on her. People usually did, as most people in the area were living hand to mouth in these hard conditions and were always glad of help themselves.

When Joyce was two, she developed rheumatic fever from an untreated streptococcus infection and was sent to the fever hospital. She was there for several months. Elsie and Mum went to visit her when the rules allowed, which was twice a week. The hospital rules were such that they couldn't pick her up, they could only look at her through a glass window. This was heart breaking for all of them, because she was so small, and looked so ill they just wanted to cuddle her. It was a hard time, particularly for a child so

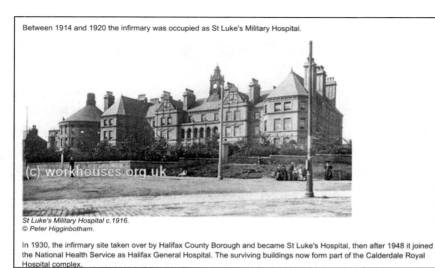

Between 1914 and 1920 the infirmary was occupied as St Luke's Military Hospital.

St Luke's Military Hospital c.1916.
© *Peter Higginbotham.*

In 1930, the infirmary site taken over by Halifax County Borough and became St Luke's Hospital, then after 1948 it joined the National Health Service as Halifax General Hospital. The surviving buildings now form part of the Calderdale Royal Hospital complex.

St Luke's Military Hospital c. 1916

small, when visiting was only at a distance twice a week. Mum was worried that Joyce wouldn't recognise them when she came home but this was unfounded, as Joyce just settled back into life with them all as if she had never been away. This illness left Joyce with a weak heart and chest problems, and as a child she often struggled with her breathing, especially in the cold and the damp. Not ideal when they were living in the inhospitable conditions in Woolshops, in a town which had

Industrial Halifax

many thick fogs during the winter.

Joyce was one of those children for whom neatness was just a natural thing. Dirt seemed to go round her or just fall off. Her clothes always seemed to fit and sit neatly on her frame, as thin and bony as she was for many years. Elsie said she always looked ready for Sunday School. Not that any of them were regular church attenders but the Salvation Army Sunday School meant a warm place to be for an hour, plus a drink and a biscuit before you went home. A rare treat for these girls. This skill for neatness and cleanliness carried on throughout Joyce's life, her home was always tidy and dust free. Even my father, who was not known for his tidiness, used to remark that Joyce kept her home spotless and yet you never saw her with a duster in her hand.

By the time Joyce came home from hospital in late spring of 1932, the conditions in the room had improved. The household income had increased, so there was a bit more money for fuel and food for them all. In the summer of 1931 Mum had started work at the milliners where she had been delivering hats. This had been a source of arguments in the household for a little while as she would only earn fifteen shillings a week (75p) as an apprentice milliner, whereas if she had worked in any of the mills, her wage would have been over twenty shillings (£1.00) a week. Mum continuously begged Elsie not to send her to the mill, and she promised to pay up all her wages and to keep doing extra jobs to help them all if she could do the job she wanted to do. Eventually, Elsie relented. I hope this was because she realised how much Mum had contributed over the past years, not only in money, but in looking after Joyce and Kathleen so that Elsie could continue to work. Mum continued to deliver some hats and run errands for the other milliners for extra money but she did give up scrubbing steps. Her hands needed to be clean and cared for to work with the fabric for hats.

Joyce's birth certificate, like Kathleen's, does not give the name of her father. Unlike Kathleen, whose father is almost certain, Elsie would never divulge the name of Joyce's father, not even to Joyce or my mother. Mum was fairly sure that he was married and that he held an important position, possibly in Crossley's factory or perhaps within the town, but she could never get her mother to tell her. This was a source of great sadness to Joyce and her family.

This seemingly endless round of looking after babies, trying to scrape enough food together to keep them fed and the constant struggle to feel warm made my mother look round at other people's lives and wonder how they coped. As a child she hadn't had time to make close friends so she didn't see the insides of other houses or what their way of life was like, but now she was beginning to get to know some of the other young women that she worked with. She wanted to feel able to meet their friends and families without feeling ashamed. Having previously seen the big houses where the mill owners lived, and the smart clothes they and their families wore, even for work, Mum knew there was a better way of life if you could only work out how to get it.

Elsie had a very broad Yorkshire accent. She spoke in dialect or factory slang and had a loud voice due to shouting across the machinery in the mill. My mother realised that the women who bought expensive hats from the hat shop spoke differently from her and her mother, for instance they didn't cut their words short and pronounced vowels carefully. Mum determined to learn to do the same, and for twopence a lesson, one of the girls in the milliner's shop gave her elocution lessons. Mum saw this as a way of getting a better job and being accepted by people who lived in the the more affluent areas. This felt to be very important in securing a better life. She ran as many errands as she could and delivered as many hats as possible to earn extra money.

Slim Pickings

You jam your heels
into the riser
paper thin soles
pressed
to the concrete step

knees bent
thighs tensed
fingers threaded into grooves
on the grey handle

   bump bump

the pram set off on its
precarious journey

   bump bump

at last the wheels roll onto the landing
manoeuvre into the room
joyless and cold

your brown-eyed sister
watches and waits
for bread or broth
a meagre offering

you are ten years old
none of this is your fault

Phyllis

Elias Marries Again

In September 1928 my grandfather, Elias, began divorce proceedings against Elsie. He had met Sarah Rutter. They both enjoyed dancing and socialising with friends so with Eliza, Elias's mother, looking after the children, they embarked on a short courtship. Elias's decree nisi came through in December 1928 and was made absolute in June 1929. Elias and Sarah were married in July 1929.

The hard times of the early thirties meant that Elias was out of work for two years early in his second marriage. He earned money by selling fish and black pudding in the pubs. The saltiness of the food encouraged customers to drink more and so he was popular with landlords. Customers would buy Elias beer, which he could put away in great quantities, however if someone added a whisky he would soon be drunk. Elias's children, Ronnie, Lola and Emmie became a part of their family, and in April 1930 Sarah gave birth to a daughter whom they called Zera Sarah Elizabeth. Her sister, Jean, was born two years later on 23 May 1932 then in November 1939 they had a son, David. The family lived at 8, Spring Lane, Greetland at this time.

Zera talked to me about her father and their family life, which she felt was a happy one, but she did say that her mother, Sarah, was strict, and could be hard on her own children and even harder on her stepchildren. The childhood for Mum's siblings was not idyllic and they all left home as soon as they were able.

Sarah was a strong character. Shortly after she and Elias were married Sarah was pregnant, not feeling at her best, and Elias was still going out in the evenings to the dog track or dancing. Sarah decided she would put a stop to this and on one particular evening Elias returned from work and went to their room to get changed. He got a shock; Sarah had cut the left leg off his best trousers! She said if he wanted to go out, he could go in his work wear, Elias would never have gone out in his work clothes and he couldn't afford to buy another pair of trousers straight away, so he started to stay home in the evenings. Eventually, when the children got older, the dancing and socialising together would begin again. The family went to Blackpool for holidays, the children being left in the boarding house while Sarah and Elias went dancing to the Tower ballroom.

The family would stay in a boarding house and in those days guests would provide their own food for the landlady to cook. Each family would have their own food cupboard in the dining room for cereals, bread, jam etc. the exception being the Sunday lunch, which the landlady cooked for everyone. It was a standing joke in the music halls of the time that landladies added 3d or 6d to the bill for the use of the cruet for the week.

Elias was also a regular in the dance halls in Halifax, being reported in the local newspapers of the time acting as Master of Ceremonies at local dances and dinners around the town. He was in great demand, very popular with the ladies and he loved the attention. He was a good-looking, well-dressed man about town, very fussy about his clothes and had highly polished shoes and spats.

One by one Mum's brother and sisters left home and found their own way in life. Sometime after 1940 Ronnie had joined the Royal Air Force. I haven't been able to find out about his RAF career, but I met him in the 1950s at my grandmother Elsie's house in Halifax. He was very good looking and charming, I guess like his father in his younger days. Lola Blanche married Alan Fairclough in January 1940 and died in April 1971.

Ronnie

Emmie left home in 1942. Emmie was 17, but only weeks away from being 18 when she signed up to join the Women's Royal Air Force. She went down to London and was about to start training when her superior officer called her to the office and told her she had received a letter from her stepmother. Sarah had written to the officer to inform her that Emmie wasn't old enough to sign up and that she should send her home. Emmie pleaded with the officer not to send her back. She told her how unhappy her home life was and how she really did want to join up. The officer had taken to Emmie and was sorry for her, so she 'mislaid' the letter until the eighteenth birthday arrived and then told Emmie that it had come to light, but of course it didn't apply now she was old enough to join up. Shortly after this Emmie and other young recruits were sent to South Wales on a training course.

They were to travel by train with all their kit. As Emmie was finding her seat, a tall young man offered to put her bag up on the rack and then took the seat next to her. They chatted all the way to Cardiff, getting on very well. He was Ronald Lampon, who was also going on a training course.

This was the start of a wartime marriage and a lifelong relationship. Emmie never went back to live with her father and his family.

Emmie and Ron Lampon in 1929

Enjoying Work and Making Friends

By the end of 1932 Mum was working at the milliners, Kathleen was at school and Joyce was looked after by either the older couple next door or by Lily, when she was not in school. Joyce was not a strong child, as the rheumatic fever had left her susceptible to frequent coughs and colds. There was no free health care, so doctors' appointments and medicine had to be paid for although there were some good-hearted doctors who halved their charges for patients living in the poorer areas. Mum would mix margarine with sugar and put it on a spoon for Joyce to suck if she couldn't stop coughing. I don't know the theory behind this remedy, but Mum used to do the same for me with butter and sugar when I was small. Mum would look after the two girls in the evenings and at weekends when Elsie was offered overtime. Elsie had left the carpet mill when Joyce was born and was working in one of the woollen mills which produced woven cloth and blankets.

Although there was an improvement in their living standards, it was still a basic existence, and they were often hungry. Kathleen was a lively energetic child who ran everywhere and used a lot of energy in everything she did. Food was still scarce; nothing was wasted and when it was gone there was nothing until the next pay day. Sometimes Thursday's teatime was dry crackers and a cup of weak tea if there was any milk left. Kathleen found this particularly hard and would walk through the market pocketing broken biscuits from the open tins on the stall or an apple which had rolled from its stand.

Some stall holders would just shout at her and chase her off, but some of them would report her to the police, and she was taken to juvenile court for theft on more than one occasion. She was just a hungry child but my Mum would have to take time off work to go to court with her and plead for her to be let off. She wasn't likely to go to prison but they couldn't afford to pay a fine either. Kathleen was never repentant, so it was Mum's way with words and her 'elocution' accent that generally persuaded the magistrate to be lenient with this young girl, who was a tomboy with plenty of spirit, and who tended to get into trouble easily. Mum worried about her and tried to keep her occupied by giving her tasks to do. Kathleen thought this was very unfair and felt that she was being picked on. The truth was that Joyce would sit and occupy herself all day without causing any trouble, but Mum needed to know where Kathleen was and what she was doing.

Mum loved working with the felt and fabrics at the milliners. She was learning to make buckram shapes for hats, to steam felt and fabric over the pro-formers and to sew hatbands to keep the hat in shape. She loved finding the appropriate ribbons for trim and making flowers from scraps to decorate the hats. She never lost this skill and throughout her life she could make a hat with fabric, fur or feathers for any occasion.

For Mum the advantage of working in a shop was that they had a half day closing, usually Wednesday. This made up for the fact that on Saturday they could be open until late into the evening. This suited Mum very well as by now she had discovered 'Tea Dances'. These were held in large halls in town and a live band played music throughout the afternoon. Men and women of all ages went to dance the afternoon away, with a cup of tea for refreshment, hence the name. Mum loved ballroom dancing, and even if she hadn't already been taught the steps she would soon pick them up by watching other dancers. This was a regular haunt for her on half days if she could make sure Kathleen and Joyce were looked after. She saved her money from running errands to pay for her entry and spent a welcome afternoon away from all the worry and responsibility.

Halifax was an industrial town, built among the hills, with many of the factories and mills down in the valley. The smoke and filth churned out by the chimneys meant that in the winter, when cloud was heavy, this smoke would get trapped and create smog which was so dense Mum used to say she could 'hardly see her hand at the end of her arm'. The smog made the buildings black and filled people's lungs with the fragments of muck trapped in the damp air. It brought an eerie silence when the buses stopped running, shops shut early and footsteps were muffled. It was a frightening atmosphere for everyone but particularly so for Mum who was worried about Kathleen and Joyce. Mum had been lost on more than one occasion when trying to weave her way through the narrow ginnels and back streets and keep her sense of direction in the suffocating atmosphere. She would carry a ball of string in her pocket, and when she felt she was getting lost she would tie one end to a railing or lamppost, so if she really did get lost she could follow the string back to a familiar landmark. She taught Kathleen and Joyce to do the same, but Kathleen was always losing her ball of string.

Getting a Council House

Women who worked with Mum talked about the new council houses which were being built in Pellon, which was not too far from the town and had a bus service. Some of them had put their names down and were being offered houses as soon as they were completed. No one knew where Mum lived, because she never let anyone come to call at the house for her, and none of her boyfriends ever walked her home.

Mum talked to Elsie about the idea of putting their names down, and Elsie agreed that a council house would make a big difference if they could afford the rent, which would be more than the room. For all their difficulties they weren't ever in debt, they went without rather than owe anyone any money. Elsie could read and write, but she was not comfortable filling in forms or dealing with officials, so Mum went to the council offices and asked if they could put their names down. She gave all their details, filled in the forms and went home to wait. There was no guarantee that they would get a new house or that it would be in the area they wanted, but anything was worth the chance of getting out of Woolshops. Much of the area had been condemned and was up for redevelopment with some of the worst buildings already being taken down. It was getting to be like living in a building site, the dust and noise was terrible.

It took another eight months, but at last they received the letter offering them a council house at 15 Rye Lane, which was out of the town centre and up towards the moor. In late

1935, when my Mum was eighteen, they finally moved into the house where they could each sleep in a proper bedroom and have a separate kitchen and a bathroom all to themselves. They had hardly any furniture, but this house was luxury beyond their dreams. A kitchen with a cooker; a sink they didn't have to get washed in; and which was big enough to take a small table and chairs, not that they had one yet, that was something to work towards. Orange boxes were still their main source of seating or a place to keep things. Two sets of windows in the sitting room made it light and airy, as well as an open fireplace with a proper hearth. Having three bedrooms meant that Mum had a bedroom to herself, the first time since she had been a baby.

With two incomes it was possible to start to buy furniture on the 'never, never'. This was a system of credit where you 'bought' an item and paid for it in small weekly amounts. Of course, by the time you had paid for one piece of furniture there was always another one needed or a replacement for an item, and so the balance never seemed to be paid up. This was why it was known as the 'never never'. They needed beds and bedding first. However basic, new beds, and new bedding were real luxuries. Elsie could get blanket seconds from the mill where she worked and with sheets that my mother bought from the market, bedtime was a treat. Money was still tight, every penny being accounted for, so when it was bath night, they used one lot of water for everyone. However, just being able to get into warm water and get washed all over in privacy was such a novelty.

Of course, there was no heating upstairs and by modern standards this was still a cold house, but there was linoleum on the kitchen and bathroom floors and with the gradual addition of rugs in other rooms this was a comfortable home. There was a coal shed, and a small garden at the back where washing could be hung out to dry. This kept the house drier and stopped mould growing on the walls, which had been a problem in the Rooming House. This was a help to Joyce and her chest problems did improve.

By the time they moved to the council house Mum was 18, Kathleen was 8 and Joyce 5. The two younger girls soon got used to living in this new environment, although to begin with Joyce wouldn't go upstairs on her own, the fear of Elsie or mum not being there when she came down took a while to wear off. However, the younger children never really felt the hardship or stigma of the Rooming House in the same way as Mum did. The girls started to go to Ling Bob school, where Joyce eventually took to playing netball.

Kathleen & Joyce, 1936

Food was still meagre and scarce. The first time a friend invited Mum to tea and gave her a scone with butter it made her sick. It was too rich, as she wasn't used to having butter on anything. Mum always felt those years in Woolshops had robbed her of a childhood. She had never had birthday parties or made a Christmas list for presents. Father Christmas wasn't ever spoken of and if there was enough food to eat over Christmas this was enough to make them content, although one thing Mum always wished for was a doll and, of course, she never got one. She talked about this, even in her old age and loved buying dolls for her granddaughters. Presents, when they existed, were necessities like gloves or a comb. The first party Mum ever had was when my brother, sister-in-law, my husband and I organised a surprise get-together for her seventieth birthday. She was thrilled when she came into the room and all her friends were there but it nearly gave Dad a nervous breakdown having to take her out for the day and keep the party secret.

Afternoon Tea

Once Mum started work, she made friends, and spent time with a group of young men and women who went dancing, walking on the moors, to the cinema and ultimately cycling. Most of the activities were inexpensive or free, and if a young man asked to take you out in those days he expected to pay for you.

Mum continued to give all her wages to her mother although most weeks Elsie would give her a small amount back for spending money, and Mum did admit to me that she didn't always tip up her extra coppers from running errands. She would use this money to buy stockings or lipstick. At that time everything in Woolworths cost sixpence, but that was each single item, so if she was buying gloves, Mum would buy one glove one weekend then go back when she had more money and hope the other one was still there.

Stockings were expensive and very fine with seams up the backs. They did ladder easily, but at least with stockings as opposed to tights, it was possible to throw one away and get another one to match. However, in warmer weather, young women would go bare legged and paint a line up the backs of their legs to represent the seam on the stocking. They often used diluted gravy browning and Mum said it was more successful if you could get someone else to do it for you, the line was straighter.

The ten years spent in the Rooming House had been hard on all of them, although Joyce was young enough for it not to have a lasting impression. Kathleen soon got used to living in a house with the benefit of security and acceptance in the community, but for Mum those ten years were something that haunted her all her life. It gave her a work ethic, and meant that she never took anything for granted, and her frugality with everything lasted throughout her life, even when she and Dad were financially secure. She valued everything she had and appreciated the effort which had gone into achieving her home and possessions. However, it also made her intolerant of people who cheated the system.

When Mum first joined the group of teenagers, she was keen on a young man called Louie, three years older than her and a trainee pharmacist. They 'walked out' on a Sunday and went with the group to the moors on bank holidays. On the way back on the bus one Sunday Louie said he was going away for a week, and some of the other young men were asking Mum if they could take her out, she was laughing and pretending to fill in her diary with dates. A quiet young man, Jeff, asked if she had a spare evening for him and so began a fifty-six year relationship.

Mum with Louie and Friends, 1936

PART 3

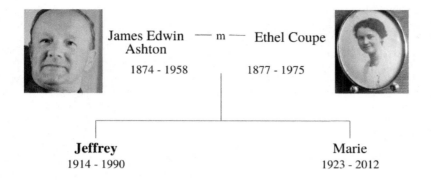

James Edwin Ashton — m — Ethel Coupe
1874 - 1958   1877 - 1975

Jeffrey
1914 - 1990

Marie
1923 - 2012

Dad's side of the family

Jeffrey Ashton, my dad, was a young chemist working at ICI in Huddersfield when he met my mother. He had been born in Halifax to Ethel and James Ashton, who had moved from Accrington in Lancashire. His mother had become a teacher specialising in maths after she left school in Oswaldtwistle, but in those days it was forbidden for married women to remain as teachers so when James and Ethel married, in July 1913, she left work and became a housewife like so many other women at that time. James had not been happy in his job in Accrington, so he applied for a clerical job at a sanitary supplies firm in Halifax. When he was offered the job they moved to Halifax and bought a two bedroomed terrace house at 5 Stafford Parade, just off Huddersfield Road.

This was where my father, Jeffrey, was born in October 1914 and, nine years later, his sister Marie. Eventually the house became too small for a growing family, and they all moved to a semi-detached house with three bedrooms at 69 Westborough Drive, where they had a small front garden and a back garden where my grandpa, could put kennels. My grandpa liked dogs and started to breed Chow-Chow. This interest helped him to cope with his dislike for the boring job he had to do under a boss he didn't like very much. He didn't make a lot of money from it, but the satisfaction of breeding healthy pups and selling them to good homes made his life more meaningful. He continued doing this until he retired in 1947.

Jeff, Age 3

Marie with one of the Chows

My grandma was one of seven children all born in Lancashire. There were four girls, Edith, Ethel, Florence, Lilian and three boys, William, Thomas and Arthur. Unfortunately Lilian, known as Lily, developed epilepsy at a young age. The treatment for epilepsy was poor in those days and fits were unpredictable, and if severe, life threatening. Initially she was treated with Potassium Bromide but in 1912 a drug called Phenobarbital became available. This drug slowed the brain function, which meant that Lily was treated as 'vulnerable' by her family and not encouraged to have an independent life of her own. She lived at home with her parents but after their father died in 1936, and the three other sisters were married, they took on the responsibility of looking after Lily and so into her old age she spent time with each of them, moving easily from one home to another.

Two months was a long time to have another person living in the house. It didn't make my grandparents home life easy, especially when my father was still at home and the dining room had to be turned into a bedroom, and my grandpa resented this intrusion into his family home. Lily had inherited money from her parents, and had a small state pension. She paid her way, but she was always there sitting reading, playing patience or, on a couple of evenings a week, going out to whist drives. She had little conversation and was very set in her daily routine. This continued until there was only Florence and my grandma left and they became too old to look after Lily so she had to go into a home. She was very bitter about this.

Dad and Marie just accepted that she appeared twice a year but

Marie and Jeff, 1926

neither of them took the trouble to get to know her very well. They had busy lives and spent very little time in the house. Grandpa was the one who felt trapped by her.   I remember her as an older woman with no insight into children, or how to talk to them. She didn't know what to say to me and just prodded me if she wanted a response. She had a very pale complexion and was thin and bony, and I found her very frightening. I feel quite guilty now as I realise how lonely she must have been. I could have played cards, read books or gone for walks with her.

Dad was a bright boy who excelled at maths and chemistry but he didn't want to go away to university. He enjoyed studying and undertook many 'correspondence courses', which were like the current day Open University, and he always passed with distinction. His work at ICI was well thought of and he was given more and more responsibility in the laboratory. The team were working on the development of nylon. I have a 'darning mushroom', which is a piece of cooled nylon from an experiment carried out by Dad and his colleague Winston. Dad had always cycled to and from school as a teenager and continued to cycle from Halifax to Huddersfield for work, up and over the hills in all weathers, protected from the rain by a yellow cycling cape and a sou'wester.

Dad was fit and keen to explore other parts of the country in his spare time. He had seen pictures of the Lake District and persuaded his friend Irvine, also a chemistry student, to cycle north to see how far they could get. One Wakes Week they set off from Halifax with a change of clothes in their panniers and a book of road maps, which was a very small scale. This was 1930 and there were very few cars on the roads, so cycling was a pleasure especially through open countryside, small villages and towns. The first time they went, they stayed in farmhouses or cottages offering accommodation to supplement a small income, but the Youth Hostel Association was just taking off. On subsequent visits they used a mixture of hostels and cottages offering Bed and Breakfast. This was a turning point in Dad's life: the landscape with lakes, rivers where he could see stones and fish in the bottom, the breathtaking mountain scenery, he couldn't believe how clear and clean the air was without the heavy industry. He was so taken with it he spent every holiday and long weekend cycling to the Lakes. He developed a passion for fishing both in rivers and from a rowing boat on Lake Windermere. Dad was competitive, and I was fascinated by the map book in which he recorded distances between the places they passed through with timings for the number of miles. He tried hard to beat his

Dad, 1935

own times each time he travelled. This worked until my mother started to go with him.

Dad's relationship with his father was never a comfortable one. He found many excuses to spend his time away from the house, his friends welcomed his company and his bike gave him a way of escaping to places he would rather be. Dad was clever, ambitious and diligent in any studying or research he undertook. He enjoyed school and work, and did well. I think my grandpa resented this as his own work life was never happy. Dad took after his mother in his academic achievements. His school reports were excellent, (unlike my own), however this seemed to irritate his father.

I stayed with my grandparents many times as I grew up but always found it strained and difficult when Auntie Lily was with them. My grandparents were more relaxed when it was just the two of them and me, they both spent time with me doing different activities. My grandpa and I would go on daily walks to the village of Warley where there were farms with dogs. He loved to see the dogs, stroke them and he even took bones from the weekend joint of meat for them. On wet days we would listen to records on the gramophone together, Grandpa being very fond of Kathleen Ferrier. Grandma on the other hand preferred Perry Como and would sing 'Catch a Falling Star' whilst dusting and tidying up. She would take me to the library or the park, and every Friday we would go into Halifax to shop and buy chocolate for the weekend. We went to the same tobacconist and bought Lindt chocolate in a wooden box to be consumed whilst watching the black and white television on Saturday evenings. Grandma would also buy a Mars bar and chop it into five equal pieces. Each afternoon when she had done her housework, made lunch and washed up, she made a cup of tea and ate one slice of Mars bar. It was her treat.

Harold and Marie's Wedding

I was eleven when my grandpa died. I missed his company and the companionable walks we had shared but I still loved to go and stay with my grandma, and did so throughout the rest of her life. She was always welcoming and was amazingly patient when I was a teenager who spent ages in the bathroom and took all day Saturday to get ready to go out with Auntie Marie and her husband, Harold, in the evening. Marie and Harold took me and my friend, Elisabeth, to the Mecca ballroom in Bradford and we had magical evenings trying out our newly learnt dance steps.

Changing jobs

By autumn 1936 Elsie, Mum, Kathleen and Joyce had settled into life in Rye Lane, Mum having worked at the milliner's full time for five years. This meant Monday to Saturday, but Wednesday was a half day to compensate for the late finish on Saturday evenings, often as late as 9.00pm. This suited Mum as she could go to the tea dances which were held on Wednesday afternoons in local dance halls. Mum had grown into an attractive, confident young woman, and was an accomplished dancer. Her mother had taught her the basic steps of the most popular ballroom dances, and she was quick to pick up new steps. She

Phyllis, Age 16

enjoyed dancing with those young men who danced well, she flirted outrageously with them all, but rarely accepted invitations to dates. However, the late hours on Saturdays irritated Dad when he was waiting to take her to the cinema in the evening, and it became a source of arguments and ill feeling. Mum knew that if she was serious about the relationship she would have to do something different.

For a while Mum stuck to her guns, but eventually she decided to change her job and went to work for Beehive Embroidery, part of Paton & Baldwins. The embroidery section was managed by the Koettlers, a German family. The business created patterns

Phyllis and Friends at Beehive

for embroidery on tablecloths, dressing table mats, and other household items. Designers created and drew up the designs, then passed them to a team of women who transcribed them onto tracery paper. This paper was then laid onto fabric and the pattern marked up with a tracing wheel. This was called thread tracing, it needed to be carried out in a good light or with a light behind the fabric. Mum learned to trace and fix patterns. She also used her selling ability and liked

Phyllis at her tracing desk

working with customers in the shop, finding the perfect item, and sometimes persuading them to buy extra pieces or complete sets of mats or cloths. Her boss claimed Mum could sell sand to Arabs, although she also used her feminine wiles to get her own way with him on many occasions. When she was working her charm to persuade him to give in to something, he would say in his German accent "and do not look at me like zat wiz zose eyes!" She would just smile, thank him profusely and feel pleased again that he recognised her worth.

With her excellent mental arithmetic she could add up a till roll with pounds, shillings, pence and half pence faster than I could have fed numbers into a calculator. She totted up the shop till roll on Monday morning and helped with the accounts. She enjoyed this work and didn't have to work late on Saturdays, which suited Dad.

Life was easier for Mum now, although she still gave her wages to Elsie to keep the household going, she did have some spending money, and she had good friends who would meet up in the pub, The Old Cock, after work. If Mum didn't have any money they would buy her a glass of beer. Mum could always make a little of anything go a very long way. One friend in particular, Mary Marr, a lovely looking blonde very lively and full of fun, had a car which made it easy for them to go out to different pubs around the district. They would go up on the moors for a walk and then call in a remote pub for a drink on the way home.

One Monday morning in 1939 everyone turned up for work to read a notice on the door which read "Closed, proprietors have left the country ". The Koettlers were German Jews and knew the war with Germany was coming.

They had packed up and gone to America. This was a shock to everyone. Mum knew that she had to find a job, any job, straight away, so they all went down to the labour exchange to be told the only work available was at Macintosh's toffee factory.

So, by lunch time Mum began her few months of factory work as a 'toffee roller', making Rolos, one of Macintosh's famous products. The women on the line were told that they could eat as many as they liked! This was a good move on the part of the company and cured the workers of wanting to eat the chocolate. They felt so sick after a couple of days they never touched them again. Mum hated this work and was constantly looking for something else, but she worked with many lovely young women who became lifelong friends, particularly Bernie.

Friends from Mackintosh's. Phyllis on the right.

Bernie had a very happy family life with her sisters, and they all took my mum to their heart. Mum stayed with them sometimes when they had been out dancing, and when Dad asked Mum to marry him, Bernie's sister offered to make her a wedding outfit. These friendships with Agnes, Mary and Bernie were very important and sustained Mum when times were hard. She always put a lot of effort into staying in touch with good friends, writing and receiving long letters from them all throughout their lives.

Violet Mackintosh (1866 – 1932)

Violet Mackintosh (nee Taylor) was born in Halifax in 1866. As a young woman she worked as a confectioner's assistant and in 1890 married John Mackintosh. In the same year, with their joint savings of £100, they opened a pastry shop in King Cross. In the early years, Violet ran the shop whilst John worked in a cotton mill.

Whilst running the shop Violet developed a recipe that combined brittle English toffee and soft American caramel. The first batch of toffee was boiled by Violet in a brass pan over her kitchen fire. Violet and John named it 'Mackintosh's celebrated toffee'. It was immensely popular and allowed the business to expand to manufacture and wholesale. By 1914 they were employing over 1000 people.

Violet held the welfare of her employees in high regard. Following John's death, she built a number of almshouses, the John Mackintosh Memorial Homes in Savile Park. Violet died in 1932 and is buried at Salterhebble Cemetery.

Holidays in the lakes

When Mum and Dad started going out together, Mum would have said that she was happier indoors in a warm comfortable place like the pictures or a tea shop. Dad had other ideas of course, and Mum soon realised that she was going to have to get used to an outdoor life. Dad was an excellent swimmer, and together with his group of friends, he liked to go up on the moors with a picnic and swim in the ponds and lakes. Dad's other interest at the time was playing chess and he wanted to teach Mum. She made a bargain with

him that if she learned to play chess then he would learn to dance. Neither of these things ever happened.

Mum couldn't swim, she'd never had either the opportunity or the money to go to the baths but Dad was sure he could teach her. 'Anyone can swim', he said. How wrong can a man be! Mum floundered and splashed, coughed and spluttered, convinced that she was drowning

Phyllis & Jeff 1933

when she was in water any deeper than her ankles. Dad gave up eventually, and left Mum sitting on the side in a bathing suit and big picture hat reading a book whilst he and his friends swam and larked about in the water all afternoon.

Dad's other love was fishing, especially in the Lake District. He bought Mum a bike for her birthday, which was at the end of May when there was a holiday week. He persuaded her that they could go to the Lakes for four days whilst Elsie was at home to look after Kathleen and Joyce. Mum had never had a holiday before, not even for a weekend, and the idea was very exciting. However, by the time she had cycled from Halifax to Keighley, she thought she would never walk again. She was not as fit or strong as Dad, and although she walked everywhere, the muscles needed for riding a bike were quite different. It took several weekends of going on shorter rides and practising on the hills around Halifax before Mum felt she could set off on a journey as long as the 82 miles to the Lakes.

Eventually the day arrived, and with saddlebags packed and a flask of water the two of them set off on their adventure. They got as far as Skipton and stayed the night at a farmhouse. Mum's legs were tired and she was very hungry, but fortunately the farmers wife took to the young couple and fed them a lamb stew and dumplings followed by fruit crumble. This food, which seemed limitless, was a revelation to Mum and she rose the next morning determined to get to like this way of spending holidays. After a hearty breakfast they set off again and got to Windermere by evening. The weekend was dry and sunny, if not very warm, but Mum was very impressed by the beautiful scenery and the clean air. The cottages and farmhouses where they stayed were warm and they were well fed. Mum would eat anything, she hadn't had the luxury of being fussy, food was food and down it went.

However, Dad had been mollycoddled by his mother, he didn't have to eat anything he didn't like, and there was always an alternative. Consequently, he didn't eat cheese, tomatoes, onions or cheap meat. They were staying in Buttermere one weekend when the landlady, Mrs Brown, offered them steak and chips, Dad's ideal meal - until it arrived, Mrs Brown had fried tomatoes in the pan with the steak and Dad said he couldn't eat it. He passed the meat and tomatoes to Mum and she ate both pieces of steak, Dad just ate the chips. The next night Mrs Brown offered them the same again, and Dad mentioned that he didn't like tomatoes. Very obligingly Mrs Brown didn't include tomatoes, but she obviously hadn't washed the pan because the steak came flavoured with tomatoes again. Mum had two steaks for a second evening.

These holidays continued for the next two years, staying in different hostels or bed and breakfast houses, until they happened to stay with Joe and Dinah Muirhead in Ambleside. They all took to each other immediately. Joe and Dinah's cottage on Church Street was old and primitive by today's standards. There was no bathroom, and the toilet was one in a row of toilets in a shack at the bottom of the gardens. There was a large iron key to open the door and no light, just a gap at the top of the door to let in some natural light. At night you needed to carry the key, toilet paper and to take a torch, and of course if it was raining you were wrapped up in a waterproof coat, quite an expedition. Food was simple and tasty, but nothing was wasted, and cheap cuts of meat were cooked to make the best of them. Mum recognised this way of life and was pleased for her and Dad to pay their board to supplement the household. Joe worked with dynamite, blasting rock in the slate mine in Langdale. His hands were pitted with slate dust. Dinah cleaned at the Vale Hotel in Ambleside. They were a kind couple who had very little but would share whatever they had with friends and neighbours, and they always seemed contented with life.

Joe was a keen fisherman and was delighted to have someone to go fishing with. He and Dad would stand together in one of the rivers when it was coming dark, hoping to bring home something for tea the following day. Joe had a little dog called Scottie who would go with them and spend the evening chasing round the fields after rabbits.

There was just one thing that put a damper on these holidays and that was Mum's inability to ride her bike safely. There were very few cars on the road but if one came in the opposite direction, she would veer towards it and Dad had to intercept. When they were riding down steep hills, if there was a bridge at the bottom Mum would lose her balance and hit the bridge or scrape herself or the bike on the stones. Dad decided to put a stop to this, so he sold Mum's bike and bought a tandem. That way he knew where she was and that she was safe.

Mum with the tandem

The other thing Dad bought was a second-hand rowing boat to keep on the shore of Windermere at Waterhead. This was shared between him, and Joe and it meant that Joe could go fishing when he wanted when Dad wasn't there.

In later years I learnt to row the boat and became proficient in steering and landing. Mum liked to sit and read and was happy for me to row whilst Dad fished.

Rowing boats at Waterhead

The War Years

Mum and Dad were married on Easter Saturday, 8th April 1939 at St Mary's Roman Catholic Church, Halifax by Father William McShane. Dad's family were strong Catholics so Mum had been going to religious instruction classes to convert to Roman Catholicism. It was a very simple wedding with very few guests. There was mass in church followed by a ham tea and scones in a cafe in town. Dad's friend Irvine was his best man and Mum's friend Bernie her attendant. Mum wore a pale blue dress and a jacket with scalloped edges that Bernie's sister had made for her.

Both mothers came to the wedding but not their fathers, and there were no photographs, because three weeks before the wedding Mum's had been in terrible pain from gum disease. She couldn't afford to go to a private dentist so she went to the community clinic dentist. He said all he could do was to take all her teeth out and have some false teeth made for her. In the meantime she had temporary teeth which she said were grey and shapeless and made her look like a horse. For their honeymoon Mum and Dad went to the Lakes, although they couldn't stay with Joe and Dinah this time as Dinah had just given birth to a little boy. They stayed in another cottage further up Church Street. They returned after a week to live in their bungalow in Southowram.

Mum had been to Dad's home many times for tea over the years and got on well with his mum and sister Marie, but his dad was much harder to please. He never spoke directly to

Mum and when he referred to her he called her 'that girl'. This lasted until I was born in 1947 and then, apparently, he was smitten and wanted me at their house as often as possible, so he started talking to Mum, calling her by her name and spending time in her company. I'm not sure she ever really forgave him for his attitude, but she was pleased to have a convivial atmosphere in their house and pleased it made life easier for my grandma of whom Mum was very fond.

In 1940 men were signing up to go to war and women were, once again, taking on the work that men had traditionally been doing. Coal was still the main source of heating and power and the Coal Office in Halifax was advertising jobs in sales and accounts, so Mum applied and was taken on to work in the shop and office. She worked here throughout the war. Her employers were supportive when she became an Air Raid Patrol Warden, (ARP). Both she and Dad took their turn in the shelters at night and helped people to get to safety during air raids. Sometimes they would work all day, be in the shelters throughout the night and then go back to work the following day. However, Mum said that there was often a lighthearted atmosphere in the shelters with singing and chatter most of the time, so it was not hard to stay awake and then go on to the day job. There was rationing and food shortages but Mum was used to making meals with very little, and she said powdered egg made the best cakes and scones.

Dad's work was a reserved occupation during the war, so he wasn't allowed to sign up to fight. Mum never knew exactly what he did but ICI kept him busy. One afternoon Mum was at home when there was a knock at the door and two dark suited men arrived in a big black car and handed Dad over to her. He was in a very dazed state, but they just said he had been unwell at work. Dad was told they would pick him up at 8.30 the following morning and off they went. The following day, despite him not being completely well, they collected him, took him to work in Huddersfield for the day and brought him home again in the evening. ICI wouldn't permit him to stay away from work so he was taxied back and forth each day. Dad just told Mum he had been a bit dizzy and they didn't want him riding his bike. This continued for three days until Dad seemed to have recovered. He went back to riding his bike and would never say what it was that had made him dizzy but Mum suspected it had been a leak of gas or chemicals as part of the war work and it was to be kept top secret.

Halifax wasn't under regular attack during the war, but northern ports such as Liverpool and Hull were targeted frequently. However, on Friday 22 November 1940, a week after the Luftwaffe attack on Coventry, a lone bomber dropped a 100kg bomb on houses in Hanson Lane in Pellon. This attack killed 11 civilians and injured a further 10 people. The bomb hit the pavement in front of house no 77.

Bomb site on Hanson Lane, 1940

The bomb fell just before 9pm. The randomness of the deaths is still shocking even after all these years; three of the dead were customers having a pint in a pub, while 16 year old Eric Pearson was killed as he waited for a bus. Today there is a 'memorial garden 'at the site, but nothing stating what happened or to explain what the garden is commemorating.

This event shocked everyone, and as it was in the area of town where Elsie, Kathleen and Joyce lived, Mum was very concerned that they observe the blackout rules and go to the shelters if there were air raid sirens. Again, it was Kathleen that she was most concerned about, because she was not known for following the rules.

Apart from this, Mum and her friends carried on their working lives and most of their social lives as they had done before, as long as they observed the blackout. Several of her friends had husbands or boyfriends who were serving in the army, most of whom came home safely but Bernie's husband, George, was seriously injured in France and Bernie went to live in France to help to nurse George and help with his recovery, as he had lost the sight of one eye and had suffered other life changing injuries. Bernie had two children in France, John and Elisabeth.

When the war ended men came back home looking for work. The women who had been doing their jobs were made redundant, and so Mum lost her job at the coal office in 1945.

Dad was delighted and said "now we can have a dog and a child". Mum soon became pregnant but, sadly, she had a miscarriage at three months. They were both very upset, however the doctor reassured them that there was no reason why they couldn't have further pregnancies. They bought a puppy, an English Setter, which Mum could look after during the day. A few months later Mum was expecting again, she was heavily pregnant in the winter of 1947 and they were still living in a bungalow in Southowram. It was a very bad winter, and the snow drifted in the windy conditions to the point that it reached up to the roof at the front of the bungalow. Mum described opening the front door to a wall of white. Dad tunnelled a way out to the footpath and managed to walk and ride his bike to get him to work but it took a long time and was very tiring. All the roads were feet deep in snow, and there were no buses. I was born on 7 April 1947, three weeks late according to my mother, I claimed I was waiting for the weather to improve. The photo below shows how deep the snow was in many parts of Halifax.

Halifax, winter 1947

Mum's pregnancy had put paid to holidays in the Lakes as she couldn't ride a bike. Her poor nourishment as a child had left her weak and she struggled with sickness and low energy in pregnancy. Dad missed his fishing in Lake Windermere but soon he had a plan. When an advert appeared in a national newspaper for a job in Staveley in the Lakes they decided that he should apply. Mum had mixed feelings about this. She would be very sad to leave her friends and family but a new start was attractive. Both sets of parents had moved from their family homes to new towns in search of work and it seemed a natural thing to do.

Life Post War

On 20th May 1944 Elsie married a man called Tom Abram. Tom was a quiet, kind man who worked as a labourer at the gas works. He looked after Elsie and brought another wage into the house. This allowed Mum to step back from her responsibilities to her mother and sisters. Tom moved into Rye Lane with Elsie, Kathleen and Joyce. Mum was very grateful to Tom for the care he gave to them all. Tom died in the autumn of 1965.

Elsie married her third husband, Arthur Greenwood, in 1969 and he persuaded Elsie to stop working in the mill now that he could look after her. Elsie and Arthur were both 72 by this time and, after a honeymoon in Blackpool, Elsie moved to live with Arthur in his flat. Elsie died in 1977 and Arthur in 1982.

Mum had continued to give Elsie money from her wages even after she was married to Dad. She felt she needed to make life easier for Joyce and Kathleen so she made a contribution until Kathleen was old enough to go to work. It was a source of irritation between Mum and Kathleen that Elsie made Kathleen work in the mill so that Mum didn't have to pay so much to the household income. Kathleen

Kathleen and Gordon

knew that Elsie had let Mum work in the milliners despite the lower wages. However, even when Kathleen got married Mum contributed to the wedding costs. Kathleen wanted a white dress and all the trimmings, none of which my mother had, but Mum helped to pay for this for Kathleen.

Kathleen met Harry Gordon Moore, known as Gordon, and married him in January 1947 when she was 19. They went to live in Accrington where Gordon ran a bakery. They had eight children, the eldest of whom was a girl, Doreen, born in the same year as me.

Five of Kathleen & Gordon's Children

I remember visiting them in Accrington, the wonderful smell of freshly baked bread and Doreen, Roger and I playing in the street.

Mum lost track of Kathleen and her family for a while, although they did write to each other from time to time. Kathleen and Gordon went to live in South Africa for some years but returned to live in the Cotswolds where they both died.

The family lived on Queen Street in Halifax for a time and I remember visiting the neat house and playing with the two boys who were so alike I could never work out which one was which. Joyce was just as neat and tidy in her own home as she had been as a child, Mum always admired her ability to look dressed and ready for anything at all times of the day.

Joyce continued to live in Halifax, stayed close to her mother and kept an eye on Elsie and Arthur in their last years.

Mum and Joyce were in regular contact throughout their lives, even though for a while it was through letters. When Joyce and Eric moved to Little Eccleston, Mum and I would visit them several times a year. It was a lovely situation by the river and with a very handy pub across the road.

Joyce met and married Eric Turner. They had twin boys.

PART 4

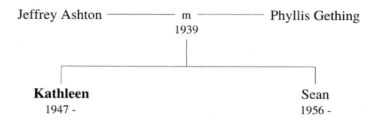

Jeffrey Ashton ———— m ———— Phyllis Gething
1939

Kathleen   Sean
1947 -   1956 -

A Big Adventure

Dad was invited for an interview at the firm, Kentmere Ltd, and was delighted to be offered the job despite the fact that the salary was only just over half of what he earned at ICI. It was an opportunity to use both his skills as a chemist and his interest in photography to develop photographic paper for

Kentmere Ltd. Mill

the future. Mostly, it meant he could live in a part of the country he had grown to love. The firm were based in the village of Staveley at the lower end of the Kentmere valley, in what was the county of Westmorland, now called Cumbria. ICI gave him a good reference and he was soon planning his new career.

There were three different departments to the company. They made box cartons for packaging goods from shoes to biscuits for a range of production companies around the country and abroad; a printing department took in work for typeset printing, and a photographic department coated black and white paper, particularly for the government but also for sale to photographers at home and abroad. They wanted to build up the photographic area and experiment with colour papers and Dad was keen to take on this challenge.

He was looking forward to working with people from other photographic companies, like Kodak or Ilford, to exchange ideas and produce different colours and finishes. Dad had a camera and took photographs all the time, we had many identical photographs around the house in both black & white and colour, in gloss, matt or other finished effects. Dad used local areas for all his research work, taking photographs around the house, garden and village. He developed the films on different papers and in different finishes in his laboratory at work. Some of the early colour trials were of Mum with a vase of colourful flowers.

In September 1948 they packed up their few belongings, including the dog and me, rode in the removal van and went to live with Joe and Dinah in Church Street, Ambleside until they could find a house to rent for themselves. It was a bit of a squash in the small cottage as Joe and Dinah now had a little boy, Malcolm, who was nine. The cottage was the largest one in the row, it had two rooms downstairs. There was no indoor bathroom. The kitchen was small but there was a scullery at the back of the house which housed the wash tub and mangle and where the large tin bath was kept. This bath was put on the stone flags, filled with water and it was where we all took our turn to get bathed on bath night. The water soon went cold, and it was a relief to get out and be wrapped in a towel. The toilet was still a bit of a trek, in a row of earth closets beyond the cottage garden; a torch was required in the dark and the door to the toilet didn't touch at the top or the bottom, so it let in all the draughts. You didn't linger any longer than necessary. However, Mum and Dad were very grateful to Joe and Dinah for their hospitality and I suspect Mum was more used to coping with just the basics than Dad was.

We stayed there for several months. Mum took me to the local baby clinic and met other young mothers with small children, in particular Amy Gibb who lived at Rydal.

......

"Amy and Phyll became friends when we lived briefly in Ambleside and then in Rydal. Phyll and Jeff were living at Ashley Green at the time. Phyll was such a lovely person, warm and friendly and with a good sense of humour. Amy and I were very fond of her." Ralph

......

Renting houses in the Lakes was comparatively expensive even then. Eventually they found part of a very large house, Ashley Green, which had been divided into three. We rented the part on the right in this photograph, mostly hidden behind the trees. The house was on the road to Skelwith Bridge, raised up on the side of Loughrigg Fell.

Ashley Green 1948

The rooms were large, and had high ceilings and floors tiled in black and white. We had lovely neighbours and a garden which led up onto the fell-side. Dad rode his bike into Ambleside then caught the bus to Staveley, Mum kept house in lovely surroundings and looked after me. The contrast of this way of life from the days in Woolshops was so great that Mum used to say she had to pinch herself daily to make sure it wasn't a dream.

Several times a week we would catch the bus into Ambleside to shop or visit Dinah. The bus, which came from Coniston, picked up a young woman, Kay Callaghan, and her daughters in Skelwith Bridge. Mum and Kay were the same age, both had small children, so they soon formed a close friendship and spent time getting to know each other with lots of coffee and laughter. Kay's daughter, Kerry, and I played together in these pre-school days and

Phyllis & Kathleen

later we stayed with each other at weekends. I loved going to Skelwith Bridge to be part of a larger family with Kerry, her sister Judith, brother Patrick, Kay and Dan. Their friendship and generosity meant a great deal to me as an only child in a house where young visitors were few and far between.

......

"I first met Phyllis – Aunty Phyll in 1950. She became my mum's best friend when they both caught the bus to Ambleside every day, and when Kathleen and I became friends. Whenever Aunty Phyll looked after me at Gowan Cottage, for lunch, she always gave me mashed potatoes and a poached egg – happy days."
Kerry

......

The first two years passed happily with family visiting from Halifax, grandparents and aunts were impressed with the scenery and the country life. Mum enjoyed being able to entertain them all in these pleasant surroundings and planned days out for them exploring the area on buses and trains. However, the savings which my parents had brought with them were disappearing fast on rent, we couldn't afford a car and in 1951 Dad was beginning to think that it had all been a mistake. They were only just keeping their heads above water financially and I was due to start school. Dad wrote to ICI to ask if they would take him on again if he went back to Halifax. ICI offered him a job straight away, so he went to tell Kentmere that, regretfully, he would have to leave.

The firm didn't want to lose him, the photographic department was growing and beginning to take shape, and so they made him an offer of a salary rise and offered to buy a house for him to rent in the village. That clinched it for Dad. Kentmere gave him the choice of two houses in the village that were on the market. One was a modern semi-detached, the other a larger, old and rather crumbling detached house with a cellar which stood in a large garden. That was the one he chose. We had a big dog, an English Setter, Lassie, and having a garden was good for keeping both the dog and me happy, although the dog did occasionally escape through the hedge at the bottom of the garden into the river Gowan. Much later I used this route to talk to the children from across the river.

When we first went to look at the house, I couldn't believe we were actually going to live there. As a child, it was one of the most frightening things I can remember. None of the rooms seemed habitable, there was dark, stained wood and dirty wallpaper was peeling off everywhere. The windows were dirty, so the house felt dark and the people living in there must have chain-smoked, the whole house smelt strongly of smoke which I should have been used to, because my parents smoked. There were cobwebs with spiders and woodlice in every corner. The rooms were different sizes with a mix of high and low ceilings.

However, Dad was a capable, practical man, and he was sure he could decorate, paint and mend to make it bright and cosy. Mum had misgivings and didn't really want to move to live in the village, but life had taught her that sometimes you just have to buckle down and put up with what you've got. She was always good at making the best of things and creating something habitable from almost nothing. Mum was no seamstress, but she had an eye for colour and could always find a way to brighten up a room.

Before we actually moved in, the house had to be scrubbed from top to bottom. A huge task, but made much easier by the support, kindness and never-failing hard work put in by Mum's friend, Kay, who arrived by bus several times a week with rubber gloves and cleaning materials and helped Mum to scrub the large house from top to bottom to make it fit to live in. They discovered

Kay Callaghan

light paint under dark and attractive tiled floors under grimy ones. Together they painted walls to brighten the dark rooms. They spent happy days together, sharing a simple lunch and laughing whilst they tackled the dirt. Mum didn't have curtains for such big bay windows, and the small windows had deep window seats so curtains had to be shortened, and cushions needed to be made for the seats. Kay sourced yards and yards of material, and between them they made curtains to keep the out the cold and cushions to provide seating. We had very little furniture at this time. Mum never forgot all this kindness, she was grateful for this friendship and support that made some very dark days bearable. Kay was a lifelong friend and a valued part of Mum's life.

We eventually moved into the house in September 1951. I don't know why neither Mum nor Dad had noticed the location before, but on our second night in the house we realised that we were next door to the village fire station. When the bell rang it seemed to shake our house.

Gowan Cottage

The house, Gowan Cottage, had been built at different times over centuries, the oldest part had very thick, uneven walls. Underneath the old part of the house there was a cellar, which consisted of two rooms with a range. The fire was raised from the floor and there were ovens at either side which heated to varying temperatures. Stone steps led to the ground floor, which also had two rooms, and then further steps led to a first floor which had been just one big room. An additional large sitting room with a bedroom above had been added in the nineteenth century and partition walls made the upstairs into three bedrooms and a storage cupboard. In the early twentieth century the occupants had built a single brick kitchen, bathroom and coal house at the back. The house was cold and damp, but Dad worked to insulate pipes, install wall heaters and make it as comfortable as possible.

Central heating was not common in many houses in those days; a coal fire was the usual way to heat up a room. Our house was never warm, but gradually, with heaters in the kitchen and bathroom, and the change from coal fires to electric ones and draught excluders, we managed to keep it at a reasonable temperature most of the time. When I became too old to get dressed downstairs in front of the fire, I was given a small electric fire for my bedroom. I often slept with my underwear between the blankets, as it prevented it from going damp overnight. Sometimes I would warm items of clothing in front of the small fire until the steam stopped rising, then I would know the clothes were dry enough to put on. However, my thick, wool school gym slip often had a cold, damp feel in the winter.

Life in Staveley

Dad gradually improved the house and Mum found pieces of furniture in the local antique shop to fill some of the corners in such a comparatively large house. She would go into the shop every two or three weeks to see what was new and if a piece came in that Mrs Coulthwaite thought might interest Mum, she would walk round to the house and let her know. Mum bought occasional tables and vases for dark corners to hold the flowers which Dad grew to brighten the rooms. Mum had a love of brass and copper, which she polished regularly. She hung horse brasses on the walls going up the stairs and mirrors with brass frames over fireplaces to reflect the light. Copper vases were filled with dried hydrangea heads and set against plain, pale walls in the front hall and upstairs on the landing. She bought an Indian table with heavily carved legs and a highly decorated brass top, which glinted as the sun hit the bright surface.

Dad found a solution for the cold damp beds by making a 'bed warmer' with large biscuit tin, a lightbulb and a length of cable to plug into the light socket. This concoction was put in my bed a short time before bedtime and at least the bedclothes weren't so cold and damp when I crept into bed with my old stone hot water bottle. Bath nights were worst, the iron bath took all the heat out of the water, and it was a race to get dry and dressed whilst there was some heat in the room.

The garden was big with old fruit trees, overgrown shrubs and bushes which ran the length of the garden, bordering the river Gowan. Sorting all this out took most of the weekends and evenings for several summers. Dad developed large flower beds and grew lupins, gladioli and chrysanthemums which Mum put in vases throughout the house. A large greenhouse stood in the lower part of the garden, so Dad used this to propagate flowers and vegetables, he built cold frames and started to grow soft fruit, particularly strawberries. We kept hens and had fresh eggs, although the original idea of killing the hens to eat was too hard to think about and never happened. Chicken was an expensive meat in those days, but we became too fond of the hens to eat them. When we had a glut of eggs Mum would sell them to the neighbours. She would hang a sign on the back gate when the hens were laying, and villagers would come and knock on the back door with an empty egg box ready to be filled.

Mum eventually made friends in the village, partly through using the local shops for vegetables and meat, but also through chatting to other mothers whilst standing at the school entrance. She would invite friends in for coffee in the morning on their way back from their daily shopping trips. The days were filled with shopping, cooking and cleaning, which Mum did cheerfully whilst listening to the radio and singing her old favourite songs, which she had danced to in the tea dances. Housework really was work in those days. We didn't have a washing machine; Mum would handwash our clothes every day and hang them out on the line whenever possible. It was during these times when I was at home that Mum would tell me about her life as a child and how hard it had been for her growing up in such poverty.

We couldn't afford a fridge so Mum would go shopping every day, bringing home just enough fresh meat and vegetables to see us through the day. Milk or cream would be put on the cellar steps where it was cool, and jelly was set down here well covered to keep insects away. Mum brushed the carpets and linoleum floors and swept them with a carpet sweeper, we didn't have a vacuum cleaner for a long time. Beds were changed weekly, and the bedding was sent to the laundry and returned, all neatly ironed, by the travelling laundry van. Mum did her own ironing on a card table for a long time until she could afford an ironing board although she always said she preferred the table to an ironing board. At weekends we travelled to Ambleside to see Dinah and Joe. Dad went fishing with Joe as often as he could. Sometimes we went through to Skelwith Bridge to stay with Kay's family.

Dad was meticulous in everything that he did. He took to making shelves and small pieces of furniture in the cellar. He would light a fire in the big range and spend winter weekends sawing and planing pieces of wood for bookcases, low tables and shelves for ornaments. He liked working with oak but sometimes he also used softer woods, it depended on what he could get from the woodyards. He made beautiful dove-tail joints, knew how to join planks with dowels and cut and chamfer table tops and legs. He would French polish the wood to make it shine. He made a small bookshelf for my bedroom, where I kept my full collection of Beatrix Potter books and Arthur Ransome stories. I still have the bookcase.

What we hadn't realised until one wet winter's day, was that when the river filled up it flooded under the stone flags and into the cellar. Dad and I were in the cellar one winter day when he saw the wet flags and accused me of spilling water on the floor, I told him I hadn't and, as we stood and watched, the water from the river began rising. We rushed to lift as much from the floor as we could and put it on the stone steps or the large stone work bench. The water came up a good two feet into the cellar and had to be cleaned and dried out after the flood before it could be used again. However, once we knew about this we just watched the forecast and planned for the flood. Eventually the river authority had a flood prevention scheme which eased this situation.

For many years there was no grocer's shop in the village so Mum posted her order book to 'Joe Holmes Grocers' in Ambleside and Joe sent the boxed order on a pre-arranged bus for us to collect at the bus stop. It was the nineteen fifties version of 'click and collect'. This seemed a very easy arrangement and bus drivers at that time were used to delivering more than people. We didn't have a telephone at home, so outgoing phone calls were made from the village telephone box and, occasionally, incoming calls were received from a friend or relative at an agreed time, hoping that there was no one else in the box at that time! I remember when the dog became ill, Mum had to queue outside the box for what seemed like a very long time for someone to finish a conversation before she could ring the vet. When he finally came, he had to put the dog down and that was a very sad day.

Dad found the adjustment to village life easy whereas Mum missed the access to shops, cinemas, her old friends and family. Dad was not keen on Mum going out on her own in the evenings, and we didn't have a television until 1958, so the evenings were spent reading, playing cards or listening to the radio. Dad took a Radio Engineering correspondence course by post, another forerunner of the Open University, and spent his winter evenings studying, eventually building radios and televisions. His brother-in-law Harold had a television rental shop in Halifax, and he would bring old, broken sets for dad to cobble together into a decent one. Dad became known around the village for his skill with TVs and was often called upon to mend or tune neighbours' sets.

Once, when Dad was in hospital, a neighbour came to ask if Dad could have a look at her TV as the picture was spinning round and round. Mum explained Dad wasn't at home but said she would take a look, as she had spent many evenings watching Dad build and repair sets. When Mum looked at the set she recognised the fault as 'a horizontal hold slippage'. Mum found the right knob at the back of the set and turned it until the picture came back and stayed still. The neighbour was so impressed she told everyone in the village how clever Mrs Ashton was and how she could mend TVs. It tickled Mum and Dad for a long time.

Money was tight but for Dad just living in the countryside was like being on holiday. We had days out on the bus and took picnics to eat by the lakeside. At that time it was possible to buy a weekly 'Rover ticket' which allowed you to travel everyday for a week, change buses throughout the day and plan your own routes without having to pay each time. Dad would plan days out in different directions, one day towards Keswick via Grasmere or Rydal, another day we would go to Grange and Ulverston. I liked it when we went to Morecambe and sat by the sea with fish and chips. My paternal grandparents would go to Morecambe for one week's holiday each year, and we would travel down by bus to meet them and walk along the front where they would buy me candy floss or Morecambe rock.

Sometimes we would just go out in the rowing boat and eat our picnic on the far side of the lake. These sound like very simple pleasures today, but they were stress free and interesting. We took long local walks through the woods and up and down the nearby hills. Dad taught me the names of the birds, trees and flowers, and we watched voles and mice making nests by the riverbank. I learnt a lot of natural history on those trips.

Friends from Manchester who had a car and two boys, came to visit regularly, and somehow, we would squeeze all seven of us into the car and go to Keswick or Cockermouth. There were no seatbelts in those days and we just squashed in where we could. Madge would bring a picnic of hard-boiled eggs, pork pie, egg sandwiches and homemade cake.

Mum would provide hot drinks in flasks. These were feasts indeed, I remember Madge's packed picnic basket with great fondness.

My brother, Sean, was born when I was nine, so life changed significantly again. Mum was fully occupied at home for the following five years. I started secondary school and made new friends, one of whom had a very sick mother. Mum would encourage my friend Dorothy to come and stay.

......

"Phyll was one of the kindest people I ever knew. I met her when Kathleen and I became best friends at High School. Always smiling, always immaculately dressed, and always full of fun. When my mother was in hospital, Phyll bought her some 'Worth' perfume, which was a dream come true for my mum. She could never have afforded such a thing herself, and when my mum died, aged 37, I found the bottle in a drawer amongst her clothes." Dorothy

......

Dad was working with chemists from Kodak and Ilford and sometimes had to go to London for meetings. When Sean was small, Mum couldn't go with him, so when I was fourteen, he offered to take me for the three days. I was so excited, this seemed like such an adventure. We travelled by train and stayed in a hotel, The Russell Hotel in Russell Square. It was November, and when we got off the train, we found London engulfed in thick fog with no taxis running. I had never seen this type of smog before but Dad was familiar with it, having coped with it in Halifax as a young man, so we went to the cinema on the station and stayed there for three hours until the fog cleared. I don't remember what the film was but it helped to pass the time. Dad was working, but we did have time to see some of the sites, like Buckingham Palace and the Tower of London before we went home. I was impressed by the architecture and the size of the river Thames. We went to the theatre to see a Brian Rix farce which Dad found very funny so that was a good evening too. Dad couldn't wait to get on the train back north, but I had enjoyed my trip to the capital.

When Mum was in her late forties she developed alopecia, diagnosed as a part of the menopause. The local GP recommended 'radio-active' treatment. A phial of 'radio-active' liquid was sent from Manchester by train to Staveley station every week for two months. Mum had to collect it from the train as none of the station staff would touch it. She took it to the doctor, who was gowned and gloved and wearing a heavy mask. He proceeded to pour the liquid over Mum's head, cover it with a plastic cap and send her home. I don't know whether this was what made her hair grow back but eventually it did. In the meantime, Mum used her millinery skills and made hats to wear with all her outfits when she went out.

Eventually life changed and I would stay in with my younger brother whilst Mum and Dad had an evening out. They would walk down the village to the local pub, The Eagle and Child and have a drink with friends.

......

"We remember playing darts on Sunday evenings at The Eagle and Child, Phyll and Jeff were regular attendees. Phyllis found it a problem letting go of the arrows. Happy days." Dorothy & George

I was eighteen when Dad inherited some money from his uncle Stephen, who had died childless. He spent this money on learning to drive and buying a car. This opened up many opportunities for holidays for my parents and brother, but I had grown out of wanting to go with them.

After Dad had learned to drive, passing his test on the second attempt, Mum decided she would like to learn. It took rather longer for her to pass her test, seven attempts in fact. The driving instructor said she could drive perfectly well, but when it came to her test she was always nervous and made silly mistakes. In typical 'Mum style' she didn't give up though, but persevered until finally the tester said 'yes, she had passed'. I think this scared her more than taking the tests, as she could finally take a car out on her own and I think she found that daunting. Despite one or two scrapes, particularly when taking tight corners on country roads, she did drive into her eighties, but she was never confident, and parking was always a challenge.

Mum's New Career

In 1974 Sean was eighteen and working, I had already left home so when mum came out of the back gate and bumped into a young woman, Ivy, coming up the road crying mum stopped her and asked what was wrong. Mum was always sympathetic to someone in tears. Ivy told her that she was heavily pregnant and her boss, the local pharmacist, had told her she should finish work, as standing on her feet all day wasn't good for her blood pressure. Mum was sorry for Ivy but asked her if the pharmacist, John, was looking for staff to cover the maternity leave. The shop was just across the road, no more than a two-minute walk away, and Mum was looking for something to occupy her time now there was less housework to do.

That afternoon she went to see John to ask if there was a possibility of some hours working in the shop. They agreed hours that allowed Mum to start after Dad had gone to work in the morning and be back in time to give him his lunch. This was ideal, Mum had always loved shop work. She was good with customers, enjoyed cleaning, was happy setting out goods in the shop and with the social interaction. Mum didn't tell Dad straight away. When she did he was not thrilled but she stuck out for those few hours a week, it was good for her to have something interesting to do. She had always been very organised, usually getting up about 6.30am and often cleaning and dusting before anyone else in the house was awake. She would have meals prepared before she set off to work and Dad would never be aware of any difference.

When Ivy returned to work after her maternity leave, she didn't want to work full-time so John agreed that Mum could stay on and work her mornings whilst Ivy worked in the afternoons. This continued even after Dad retired. He would garden or do house repairs whilst Mum worked, then in the afternoon they would go out together. I don't think this was exactly how Dad would have planned their lives but he took on some part-time consultancy work with the firm, and Mum was adamant that she wanted to continue to work, meet people and earn a little bit of money. Dad, in his old-fashioned way, insisted that she kept the money for herself and it gave her the independence she always craved.

In 1975 Mum and Dad became grandparents when I had my daughter Rachel. This was a role they both loved. Dad and Rachel became very close when Dad spent more time at home. They shared a sense of humour and spent time together whilst Mum was at work. Dad loved watching her grow and learn about new things around her. Sadly my brother's daughter was only 6 months old when he died.

Mum became great-grandma in 2002 when the first of her three great-grandchildren were born.

John Wood was a good friend and boss and he accommodated the staff as much as he could whenever they wanted to swop hours or take holidays, as long as the shop was covered over key hours. I'm sure Mum wheedled her way into working things round to suit herself sometimes, but she always praised John for his kindness and understanding, making the shop a pleasurable place to work and shop. During her working life she thought John was just the best pharmacist to help and support people in the village with their illnesses and problems, and she worked loyally for him for thirty years.

During John's holidays he employed locum pharmacists, and this was when Mum met Carolyn Rayner.

......

"So many happy memories of times with Phyll; in the shop, out for bar snacks, and later at the cottage. Always a welcome. I will miss her and am very grateful to have known her."
Carolyn

......

They got on like a house on fire and became good, close friends. They enjoyed working together and went out with the other staff for social evenings. Even after Mum had retired, they continued to have evenings out together and visit each other for coffee. Carolyn was a great friend and support, right up to the end of Mum's life. This friendship was very important, it meant a great deal to Mum to have someone with whom she could share social activities or go out to events in the village. Mum would meet friends in the local café and have coffee and cake, it kept her in touch with people and events in the village.

......

"Phyllis would come into the café, Staveley Antiques, we kept a sugar bowl specially for her with caster sugar, she didn't like sugar lumps. Normally we would have chocolate damson brownies, I always felt extremely guilty when we had none left. Phyllis never really wanted anything else. I will always think of

her when eating chocolate damson brownie. Always beautifully dressed, elegant and full of light." Rebecca

......

Mum liked nothing more than to go the village hall for an evening of entertainment that included Andrew Taylor and John Wood playing, singing and telling jokes.

Working became more difficult when Dad was ill and Mum had to take time away to look after him, but the other staff all helped and Mum kept her job. They had just celebrated their Golden Wedding when Dad became really unwell. He had been diagnosed with Glaucoma three years previously which was being treated with eye drops, but he worried about losing his sight. His mother had lost much of her sight and found life very difficult for the last few years of her life. The doctor thought Dad was suffering from depression on account of the glaucoma, and treated him accordingly, but when he was admitted to a private hospital in York something more serious was immediately suspected and Dad was sent for a scan. He was admitted to York District Hospital and diagnosed with lung cancer. This was a shock to all of us, and we spent the last two weeks of his life sitting with him in a hospital side ward. I worked in the NHS and knew that there were better ways of looking after terminally ill patients. I still feel sad that he had been denied a peaceful last few weeks in his own home surroundings.

Mum's job was a boon after dad died in 1990. It gave her a reason to get up, go out and continue to meet people. She felt she had a purpose to each day, and it provided stimulation and motivation to her life. She continued to work in the mornings, meet her friends in the afternoon, and then spend her evenings relaxing in front of the television.

In 1997 the rules governing pharmacy assistants changed, and in order to work with pharmaceutical products staff now had to hold the NVQ level 2 in pharmacy support. By now Mum was 80 but this didn't dampen her spirits; she set out her stall to learn about minor ailments, all

John Wood and Phyllis

the different drugs with their interactions, and undertook the different Interact modules, which she passed with flying colours. This ensured she could go on working with prescriptions and advising customers about 'pharmacy only medicines'.

Mum worked for John Wood until he retired in 2004, which meant she retired at the age of 87. John had been a friend, an excellent boss and a great support to Mum during many difficult times. She was going to miss his company and ample supply of jokes. When the new pharmacist, Anothai Chareunsy, took over the pharmacy he kept the existing staff. Mum's job had been taken on by a younger woman, however he was very curious to meet this 87-year-old woman who had just retired. Never one to miss an opportunity, Mum went to introduce herself and got on very well with Anothai and his wife, Lorna, so she continued to visit the shop regularly and made coffee for the staff when they were busy. They also became great friends. This eased the disappointment of having to retire for Mum and kept her active and socially alert for the next few years. She said John couldn't have passed the shop on to anyone better, Anothai continued to look after the village population in the same caring way and provided additional services when he was able.

Mum stayed living in Gowan Cottage after Dad died but the garden was becoming a problem. Such a big garden needed a lot of attention, cutting the grass and the hedges, looking after the old trees and keeping the flower beds tidy. Even with help from friends and neighbours it was hard to keep it in good condition. When Kentmere Ltd offered Mum a cottage on Kentmere Road, near the church, she decided to move. It was a smaller house to look after and heat, and there was only a small front garden. Moving took place over a couple of weeks, Ivy's husband, Steve, and son, Gary, helped to sort out the cellar with all Dad's woodworking tools and gardening equipment as well as a fair amount of rubbish. They had a van and transported large items across the village to the new home. There was no hurry to move everything, so Mum took smaller items across every day. She even carried her Christmas tree, fully decorated, lights and all, across to its new home.

Mum was a hoarder. She kept all sorts of 'useful' bags, boxes, rubber bands, string, plugs from long-gone equipment, wrapping paper, brown paper, envelopes and containers with sentimental value. She always wrapped food in two or three layers of plastic to keep it fresh. She believed dried orange peel kept the moths away so every drawer and wardrobe was 'scattered' with pieces of peel. Mum had clothes in wardrobes in both bedrooms, on the back of the bedroom doors and in chests of drawers in each room. She loved having clothes for every occasion, matching colours and styles to suit her mood, even if the clothes were many years old. Her weight varied in her later years, so she kept everything 'for when she was slim again', and then this or that would fit her. The lack of everything as a child made her reluctant to part with anything. She appreciated the material possessions she had come to own. She was always thrifty in her use of food, utilities and goods, believing that everything would come in useful eventually. She moved all these items with her to Scar View and continued to collect and hoard to the end of her life.

Venturing Abroad

My parents had never been abroad. Dad refused to get on an aeroplane and Mum didn't want to go on a boat, so for their holidays together they travelled throughout England, Wales and latterly, Scotland. Dad's ideal holiday was to stay in a hotel in Granton-on-Spey, go fishing with the local fishermen and gamekeepers during the day, and then sit in the bar listening to them telling tales all evening. The outdoor life in beautiful scenery with the benefit of the local people's knowledge and banter was his ideal holiday. He was never interested in high living or fancy food. Mum was happy enough to sit in a comfortable hotel, have her meals made for her, and read a book or chat to the locals, some of whom became very good friends.

Dad fishing with James

She had cards and visits from Elizabeth, Margaret and Karen Coupland all her life after she had watched the young girls grow up during their holidays in Scotland. Dad got a taste for whisky although Mum preferred a beer. However, she also took time to go to Halifax to visit friends and to Rye to see her sister Emmie, and her family and friends.

After Dad died, Mum became more adventurous and applied for a passport. She travelled to visit her sister, Emmie, in Rye every year and on the next occasion they booked a day trip to France, flying from a local airport. Mum

claimed that flying was just like getting on a bus, she never gave it a second thought. Following this experience, she went with Emmie and their two friends, Pauline and June, to Germany, however the German countryside didn't impress her, she said it was boring compared with the Lake District. This didn't stop Mum and Pauline booking a package

Phyllis and Pauline in Italy

holiday to Bruges, where they travelled by train with an old Dutchman who kept insisting they look at the cows in the fields as if they had never seen cows before.

Following on from this successful trip they became more adventurous and flew to Mallorca, where they went

Phyllis and Pauline in Italy

on bus trips through the spectacular mountain scenery and tried some of the local cuisine. Lake Garda was recommended to Mum, but the first time she went they stayed at the southern end of the lake which was pretty but none of the drama of the mountain scenery.

When they went a second time she and Pauline stayed in the north and found the beautiful mountains mesmerising, particularly in the evenings when the sunset turned them into pink marble. On subsequent trips to Italy they visited Florence, Venice and the Tuscan countryside, staying in a small hotel by the sea. Pauline had a friend who lived in Cyprus so they went to stay with her, met her family and joined in with events in the local village. They had developed a taste for warm climates. These experiences began several years of taking two foreign holidays a year and exploring Italy in particular.

Phyllis and Pauline seeking shade

When Pauline's husband became ill and couldn't be left, Mum and I started to go away for a few days together and our first trip was to Barcelona, where we used the tourist bus to take us to all the famous sights including the Cathedral, Sagrada Familia which fascinated us both with its contrast of ancient and modern architecture; then Paris where we travelled on the metro regularly, discovered restaurants where they served generous portions of Steak Frites, and sat outside and drank French beer in the sunshine people-watching and laughing at some of their behaviour. We visited Notre Dame, Eiffel Tour, the Pompidou Centre and many other famous sights. Mum was always fascinated by architecture and was impressed by the rich decorations in churches and cathedrals, although she always said that the gold would be better used to feed the poor.

Phyllis in Cyprus

David and I took her to Prague, Nice and Lake Como, from which we had a trip to Switzerland where she bought copious amounts of Swiss chocolate for gifts and then managed to leave it in the fridge in her hotel room. She loved the warmth and different experiences but wasn't always keen on the food. Garlic and rare meat were a great source of dismay, however, one of the most successful meals in the south of France was when we discovered a small cafe serving Moules Frites with a glass of white wine. Surprisingly, Mum said it brought back happy memories of eating mussels with Elsie when they were in Woolshops. Mum was 89 the last time we went abroad but she did say her passport lasted until she was 95 so there were always possibilities. I am very glad she had these opportunities, even if it was later in life, she had a thirst for exploring and loved the statues and paintings in the old buildings. Her favourite was Venice where she thought the colours and reflections in the canals were like life sized paintings. Foreign languages posed no barrier in her attempt to communicate with people, and somehow with a few words and gestures it worked. She made friends wherever she went and kept in touch with many of them until she died.

......

"I met your mum once, she was lovely, gave me sherry to drink." Sarah

Meeting More Family

Throughout most of Mum's life, she resisted having anything to do with her father's second family. She resented the easy life she thought they'd had and felt aggrieved about the opportunities they had been given in life that had been denied to her. She knew there were mixed feelings and disapproval throughout the family about the way her mother had behaved, but whatever her own views about her mother's life, my Mum always defended Elsie's decision. Mum knew that Elsie had loved them all and that she had suffered remorse and loss of contact with her children because of the drastic action she had been driven to take in 1926. Mum felt that because of this her father's side of the family wouldn't want to get to know her, and she wasn't sure she wanted to know them. She kept as much contact as she could with Emmie, Kathleen and Joyce, although she lost track of Ronnie until much later in life. Lola just got on with her own life despite the rest of them.

Mum remained angry about her father's behaviour towards her mother and his apparent lack of care for his children only to see him have a complete change of behaviour with his second wife and children. Elias had made many attempts to contact Mum when she was in her teens and twenties, he would visit her in the shop or hang about outside waiting for her to leave in the evening. He wanted to talk to her, and to try and maintain some contact with his eldest daughter. However, his second wife, Sarah, came to see

Mum at work and warned her off. Sarah told her, in front of her work colleagues, to leave her father alone, that Elias was always in a bad mood when he got home after visiting her and it upset their home life. Mum, in her typical arrogance of youth, told Sarah that 'she would do what she liked and if she wanted to see Elias she would do so'. However, she didn't want her own brother and sisters to suffer, so she did try to avoid him sometimes and curb his visits.

The Gethings became a very large family in Halifax, so Mum got to hear news about all of them over the years and I suppose they heard about her through the same channels. She did try to see her father at the end of his life, when she heard that he wasn't well. He had suffered a stroke, and so when she went to Halifax she tried to go and see him but couldn't find him in his usual haunts. She was sad not to have had the chance to talk to him one more time.

In 1991, just after Dad died, Zera, the eldest of Elias's second family, wrote to mum. She said that she and her husband, Douglas, were travelling to the Lakes in their camper-van and would like to meet up. After some initial hesitancy, Mum wrote back to Zera, said she would love to see them and invited them to park the van in the back garden of Gowan Cottage. It was a very large garden and Mum loved having company and entertaining people.

This was one of the best decisions she ever made. She, and my husband and I, got to know Zera, her sister Jean, brother David and all their families. We were able to meet family members we didn't know we had, they were a warm and welcoming family full of fun. They had led varied and interesting lives, including sailing round the world, and were pleased to let us share family events with them. It enriched all our lives. Mum spent holidays with her sister, Zera, in Weston-super-Mare and when she was too old to travel on her own, we would take her to visit them or we would all meet up somewhere centrally where we spent weekends laughing, eating and drinking in very convivial company. We met Zera and Douglas's daughter, Kathy and her musical husband, David. Kathy had lived in Switzerland for most of her adult life.

We also got to know Douglas's brother, David and his wife Catherine. We took trips to the Edinburgh Festival to see Kathy and David's musical plays on the Festival Fringe and afterwards we would all go out to eat together, David, David and David with Kathy, Cathy and Kathy, Mum and Zera thought this was hilarious. We enjoyed weddings and party celebrations together in Weston. My cousin Kathy held her fiftieth birthday party at our house in Ripon, for as many family members as could get here. Sadly, her husband, David, had died earlier in the year. It felt good to meet a wider family, for Kathy to have the support of her aunts and cousins, and for Mum to have the opportunity to discover more about her family.

Mum was always amazed to discover that having spent her early life with just herself, her mother and two sisters, she had then ended up with such a large family of brothers and sisters, nephews and nieces. For a lot of her life talking about her family was a painful, sad experience but eventually she came to recognise the love her extended family felt for her and she was able to leave some of the sadness in the past.

Mum was very proud of my brother and I, our spouses and her grandchildren and great-grandchildren. She loved telling her family, friends and acquaintances all about our achievements and showing them photographs of our exploits. When her great-grandchildren were born, she was concerned that she would die before they got to know and remember her, but she was a presence in their lives for several years and I'm sure that fear was unfounded. She enjoyed their vitality and ability to express themselves freely in the world. If she had been a young woman in the twenty first century, she would have embraced all the modern culture, she would have dyed her hair bright colours, had a discreet tattoo and kept her maiden name when she married. She was hidebound by convention and followed many accepted traditions but did rebel when she felt it was justified and was honest, if a little forthright with her opinions.

Degeneration

she looked
into the mirror
the middle
of her face was
kaleidoscope - in grey
she moved her head
up then down
her face came in
and out of focus
how could she
apply makeup now
her fingers traced
her eyelid as
the black pencil
followed slowly
seventy years of
easy beauty
now a daily
challenge

The Final Year

Mum lost family and many lifelong friends during her nineties and missed their letters and phone calls talking about the old days. She and her friend, Pauline, eventually became too old to travel to see each other but they spent hours on the phone discussing TV programmes and laughing and joking just as if they were in the same room. However, Mum had also developed strong friendships with many people in the village through her warm friendly personality and caring approach to young women and their families.

......

"Thank for being a wonderful friend to me, I used love our chats over a cuppa. You always had time to listen to me when I was a bit low and missing my family. You became my family and I am going to miss you a lot. A lady full of grace is how I will remember you." Jan

......

Several of these friends supported her with practical help and friendship during her last years and enabled Mum to live independently in her own home right up to her death.

......

"I'll miss calling in to see you on my way up and down the valley, all your stories and jokes." Maureen

......

She still enjoyed going out for lunch and was very partial to a sweet sherry and tonic water, but activities that needed good eyesight became far less enjoyable.

......

"I will miss you Phyll, calling out in a very LOUD voice at the local concerts we went to. Also tripping over your 'leg stool' at meals in local pubs. Such memories." Colin

......

The last twelve months of her life became extremely difficult and frustrating through the development of macular degeneration. It took away her ability to enjoy reading and watching television which were the two things she did regularly, particularly during the winter months. Talking newspapers and books for the blind filled some of the gaps but it was not the same as holding a book in her hands and turning the pages at her own speed. She became less confident at moving around, even in her own home and she almost gave up going out alone. She was worried about falling and breaking bones.

......

'Phyll had audio tapes delivered regularly when her eyesight got worse. They came in various coloured packages; red, blue, green and white. When they arrived, she would always say "What colour is the Audio Tape?" If I told her it was a red one she would say "Oh good, they are the naughty ones, but don't tell anyone".' Annette

......

131

Mum died in Harrogate District Hospital, with family around her, on 2nd January 2015 after spending Christmas with us all in Yorkshire.

Adrift

We never said goodbye
my mother and I
we sit in the ambulance
holding hands   making plans
talk of tomorrow
we both know this is not
the way it will be
I listen to calm voices
of paramedics   reassuring
and I look out of the window
at grey light and bare trees
the very depth of winter.

The hospital bed is too big
the bedclothes too flimsy
I slide my hand under the sheet
so your warm fingers
as light as a bird's wing
can rest untroubled in mine
I tell you the things we are doing
the bustle of our lives
whilst you lie silent   undecided
your breath as light as thistledown
slow as dreams
and I am adrift.

Superstitions

My grandmother, Elsie, was very superstitious and, despite what her daughters said about it, they also inherited some of these beliefs. I have observed them commenting on many of these over the years. Some of the most frequent ones were:

- Crossed knives on the dining table mean you'll have a row
- If you drop a knife there will soon be a man at your door
- If you drop a teaspoon a lady will be coming to visit
- Looking at a new moon through glass will bring you bad luck
- Never wear pearls, they'll bring you tears
- Opals are bad luck and bring a broken relationship
- Never bring white lilac into the house, it brings bad luck
- A bird on your windowsill or tapping on the window means a death in the family
- If someone drops a glove and you pick it up you will soon receive a present
- If you pick up a pin or a penny you will have good luck
- Never put red and white flowers together, it will mean an illness
- A horseshoe on your door will collect good luck but if it reverses the good luck will run out
- A visitor should go out of the same door they came in
- Never open an umbrella indoors, it offends the sun
- A four leafed clover brings good luck, it is said Eve took a four leafed clover out of the Garden of Eden with her
- A right handed itchy palm means money coming in but on the left hand it means money going out

- Spilled salt should be thrown over the left shoulder
- Black cats, broken mirrors, thirteen at a table and walking under ladders are all bad luck

There seemed to be a superstition attached to almost everything we did, the last time I visited Joyce she dropped a teaspoon and repeated the superstition, then she laughed and said "but then you are already here" as if the superstition were true.

Thank You!

Thank you to the following people and organisations who have helped with recollections, information and photographs. All of these have contributed to the realisation of this biographical story of my mother, grandmother and their wider family.

- Archive of Calderdale History
- Old Photos of Halifax
- Photographs from Malcolm Bull's Calderdale Companion at WWW.CALDERDALECOMPANION.CO.UK
- From Weaver to Web
- News Centre, Calderdale Council
- AIRCRASHSITES.CO.UK
- Ancestry
- My husband for his support and patience with my writing and editing time
- Members of Scriveners U3A writing group for reading and commenting on the manuscript
- Edwin Rydberg (www.quantumdotpress.com)
- Sheila Whitfield for her help and support in editing the document
- Friends who wrote down their particular memories of Mum
- Zera Wilson for generously sharing information about my grandfather and her family life
- David Gething for sending information about his family

- Kathy Hönigsberg for sending information from her mother's papers
- Emma Lampon for talking to me about her early life
- Elsie Gething for talking about difficult times in her life
- Phyllis Ashton most of all for recounting the most painful experiences in order to teach me about standing up for what you believe to be right

About the Author

Kathleen was born in West Yorkshire but brought up in The Lake District. She wrote for the school magazine and enjoyed making up stories for local children and the children she cared for when she worked as an au pair in Brussels.

Having worked in the NHS in North Yorkshire for twenty-six years, where writing board papers and clinical reports were her daily routine, she promised herself that when she retired she would return to writing and storytelling for her own pleasure. She joined the local U3A Family History group and researched her mother's family back through many generations.

Her first book of poetry, Ripples Beyond the Pool, was published in 2019 and she is working on another volume for 2023. Her poems are included in a wide range of anthologies.

Kathleen still lives in North Yorkshire, and when she is not writing, she enjoys gardening, fell walking, cooking and once a week, she and her husband can be found at a class practicing Rhumba, Tango, Quickstep and Rock and Roll for fun and exercise.

She can be found online at **kateswannwriter.com**

APPENDIX

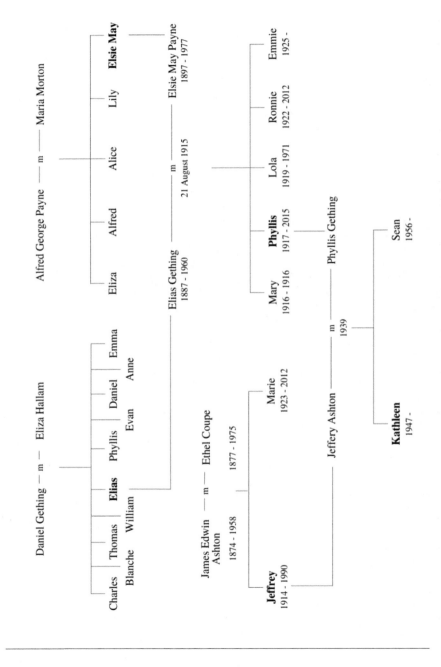

Daniel Gething — m — Eliza Hallam

Charles | Thomas | William | Phyllis | Daniel | Emma
Blanche | Elias | | | Evan | Anne

James Edwin — m — Ethel Coupe
Ashton
1874 - 1958   1877 - 1975

Marie
1923 - 2012

Jeffery Ashton

Jeffrey
1914 - 1990

Alfred George Payne — m — Maria Morton

Eliza | Alfred | Alice | Lily | Elsie May

Elias Gething   Elsie May Payne
1887 - 1960   1897 - 1977
              m
         21 August 1915

Mary   Phyllis   Lola   Ronnie   Emmie
1916 - 1916 1917 - 2015 1919 - 1971 1922 - 2012 1925 -

Phyllis Gething

              m
             1939

Kathleen   Sean
1947 -   1956 -

The car she drove

The car she dreamed of driving

A proud Grandma

A proud Great-grandma

Surprise at 70

90 years young